## Praise for *Beyond Smart*

"Insightful, lively, and ultimately practical . . . Morgan asserts that parents are their child's first and most important teachers, then shows how to make the most of that crucial role. Based on the latest brain and learning research, *Beyond Smart* offers useful tools for parents who want to help their child achieve their full potential — from cradle to college, in the classroom and beyond."

—Carol S. Dweck, Ph.D.
author of *Mindset: The New Psychology of Success*

"Every parent is a teacher — and every parent can use a teacher. Linda Morgan's accessible, practical, and wide-ranging book gives parents the skills and wisdom to teach their children well."

—Eric Liu
author of *Imagination First* and *Guiding Lights*

"This book — approachable, practical, and ultimately indispensable — is filled with valuable tools. Morgan tells parents everything they need to know — and more — about helping their child become a learner. Written in a lively, down-to-earth style, this book is required reading for parents who need simple tools for helping kids succeed in school and, ultimately, in life."

—Michele Borba, Ed.D.
author of *The Big Book of Parenting Solutions: 101 Answers to Your Everyday Challenges and Wildest Worries*

"*Beyond Smart* is engaging, brimming with insight, and immensely useful. It's a go-to book for parents who want to maximize their child's school experience. I highly recommend it."

—Michael Gurian
author of *The Purpose of Boys* and *The Wonder of Girls*

"*Beyond Smart* offers clear, straightforward guidance for parents who want to raise their children to be socially, emotionally, and academically successful. Author Linda Morgan elegantly describes the vital interplay between children's emotional and cognitive development, then translates this research into simple recipes for parent-child interaction that will help kids grow up to be safer, smarter, and kinder human beings. This book is an enjoyable read and a practical tool for busy moms and dads. My advice to readers: DO try this at home!"

— JOAN COLE DUFFELL
executive director, Committee for Children

"*Beyond Smart* is an instructional roadmap! This easy-to-read text gives contemporary information that parents can apply throughout their children's developing years. Parents want the best for their children; *Beyond Smart* should be in the hands of every parent as their children grow."

— VAUGHNETTA J. BARTON, M.S.W.
executive director, Foundation for Early Learning

"Linda Morgan promises to help you navigate the challenging terrain of learning, and she delivers. *Beyond Smart* is smart yet accessible — overflowing with pivotal insights and practical, achievable advice. It's a 'must read' for parents and others who care about children."

— REBECCA C. CORTES, PH.D.
co-author of the PATHS
(Promoting Alternative Thinking Strategies) preschool curriculum

# Beyond Smart

# Beyond Smart

## Boosting Your Child's Social, Emotional, and Academic Potential

Linda Morgan

ParentMap

Printed in the United States of America
Published by ParentMap
Distributed by Ingram Publisher Services
03 05 10 MAL 01 30 00 14 95
First Edition

Cover design: Emily Johnson
Interior design and composition: Emily Johnson
Front cover photograph: Anetta R., Photomoment, © iStock
Back cover photograph: ThomasVogel, © iStock
Library of Congress Cataloging-in-Publication Data is available.

ISBN-13: 978-0-9823454-2-9
ISBN-10: 0-9823454-2-9

ParentMap dba Gracie Enterprises
4742 42nd Ave. S.W., #399
Seattle, WA 98116-4553
206-709-9026

*ParentMap* books are available at special discounts when purchased in bulk for premiums and sales promotions, as well as for fundraisers or educational use.

Place book orders at *parentmap.com* or 206-709-9026.

SUSTAINABLE FORESTRY INITIATIVE
Label applies to the text stock
Certified Fiber Sourcing
www.sfiprogram.org

To Ariella, Sasha, and Oliver,
who are beyond sensational

# Contents

# Acknowledgments

My children, who have been the source of countless article ideas, deserve considerable credit for this book. Rarely have I needed to reach very far for material, whether exploring issues in learning, relationships, social development, or many of the other topics I address in this book. Melissa, Marty, Todd, and Wendy — thank you for your support, interest, and tolerance; through the years I've "borrowed" endless anecdotes and real-life experiences from you for my columns and features. To your occasional chagrin, you never knew when an antic or two would end up in print. A word of warning to Ariella, Sasha, and Oliver: You're next.

My mother, Frances Rogers, and my mother-in-law, Edith Morgan, were my greatest advocates and biggest fans long before I'd ever published a word. Since then, they've read — and saved — each article I've ever written. And that, I know, is way above the parental call of duty.

I'd especially like to thank Alayne Sulkin, publisher of *ParentMap.* Alayne's vision — and her extraordinary ability to make things happen — have been nothing short of inspirational. What a pleasure it's been to work with Alayne and with the smart, dynamic team at *ParentMap.* Special thanks go to Kristen Russell Dobson, top-notch editor and all-around terrific person; and Emily Johnson, art director, whose talent and infinite patience have helped make this process such a positive one. I've also been fortunate to work with Jen Betterley, who has done a Herculean job of tracking sources for this book.

My husband, Mike Morgan, has been a constant source of support and encouragement. Blessed with pitch-perfect parenting instincts, he's helped make our own parenting journey truly amazing, occasionally humbling, and altogether awesome.

Finally, to the friends and family who have cheered me on over the years, thank you. We've all been in the parenting biz together — and that has made all the difference.

# Introduction

The excitement, the wonder, and yes, the worry begin the instant you discover you're about to welcome a little person into your life. You have been blessed with a brand-new being to love, nurture, and teach.

Those of you who are up on the latest CNN reports, nightly news broadcasts, and all the noise reverberating from your legislatures will realize that much of your time and energy will be spent focused on that last activity: to teach.

It sounds simple. But we're learning that education is an ongoing process that begins the minute your child emerges from the womb (or even earlier, as some would argue) and has implications experts are only just beginning to recognize.

*Beyond Smart* explores that process in ways that speak directly to you. This book offers tips and suggestions, many from celebrated educators and child-development specialists, to help you and your child navigate a challenging terrain. I refer to "parents" throughout the book as representing not just mothers and fathers, but caretakers, aunts, uncles, grandparents — any and all of you who care for and about children.

Thanks to the latest findings in early learning research and neuroscience, we now know that the way you interact with your child during his or her early years is crucial. Big business has taken this information to heart — and to every toy outlet in the country. The plethora of products — "smart" toys and IQ-enhancing DVDs — all promise to elevate tots to new levels of learning. Not wanting to miss a beat, parents stock up on puzzles, educational software, and Baby Einstein products. Could these be the tools, parents wonder, that will propel my kids to greater heights?

What parents really crave are the skills and insights that will enable them to equip their children with the intellectual, physical, social, and emotional tools they'll need to compete and succeed in today's rapidly changing world.

We live in the "No Child Left Behind" era, when test scores are a national concern and magazines touting college rankings instill panic in parents — of preschoolers! It's a time when advances in science, technology, medicine, and business emerge from countries such as China, India, and Japan; when our own students seem to be losing ground in pivotal academic disciplines; when creating a global economy and a broad worldview has never been more essential.

What do we want for our children? Success in school — social, emotional, and academic — tops our list. We'd like them to master the art of sharing toys and dealing with cliques; to cope with many different teaching styles; to face disappointing report cards and other challenges with grace and confidence. We'd like to know when to intervene and when to stand back; how to tell if our kids are really ready for school; why our kids behave differently at school than at home; how their gender affects their learning; and much, much more.

For more than six years, I have penned a column titled "Getting School Ready" for *ParentMap,* an award-winning Seattle-area parenting magazine. Through years of education reporting, I've had the privilege of working with an extensive Pacific Northwest-based network of world-class researchers and scientists in the fields of infant brain development, emotion coaching, and cognitive development. Among the sources that I've drawn upon for this book are the University of Washington (UW), the Talaris Institute, the Gottman Institute, the Foundation for Early Learning, and the UW's Institute for Learning and Brain Sciences (I-LABS).

Studies come and go, but essential truths emerge. Based on the latest in neuroscience, educational research, and more than one hundred interviews, I present some of those truths here, along with practical tips — culled from some of the finest minds in education and child development — for applying that knowledge in your day-to-day life.

It's my sincere hope that *Beyond Smart* will help guide you through the most important issues of early childhood. You are your child's first and most important teacher. Understanding the crucial role you can play in your child's education can help him thrive — in school, and, ultimately, in life.

CHAPTER 1

# It Begins at Birth

## DEVELOP A PARENTING PLAN

Wrapped up in excitement, exhaustion, and love, most new parents don't spare a thought for their baby's eventual journey through the world of education — and why should they? The days of lunchboxes, school buses, and homework seem eons away. But long before you change your first diaper, you can begin to lay the groundwork for your child's success in school. You and your partner can take the crucial first step of getting on the same page with your parenting. And you can learn the best ways to talk to your baby, building skills that pay off in preschool and beyond.

When a couple — let's call them Jon and Jayne — discovered to their great joy that Jayne was pregnant, they did what most expectant parents do: They began planning for that very precious baby's birth. They shopped for strollers, high chairs, and cribs; they decided which prenatal classes to attend and learned how to breathe during labor.

Looking back, Jon likens that ritual to prenuptial prep. The drunk-with-love couple fashions the glorious wedding with great care and micro-attention to detail. In effect, they plan for the wedding, not the marriage.

That's pretty much the way Jon and Jayne describe their first foray into the parenting world. Both have strong, dominant personalities and backgrounds that, while similar on a socio-economic level, differ in culture. Jon's family is large, laissez-faire, and permissive. Jayne's? Hands on, strict, and demanding.

With no real parenting plan in place, Jon and Jayne ended up at odds over just about everything. "We fought over chores: Who does what for the baby and when. We fought over discipline and later, over schoolwork," remembers Jon. "Our child could see we were always on different pages." And that, he says, created even more chaos and confusion.

"We needed to present a united front," says Jayne. Eventually — and with professional help — they figured that out and had a considerably easier (and less tumultuous) experience raising their next two kids.

"It's more important that parents agree than it is to be right," says Jon. "It took a long time for me to understand this."

We've been told for decades that it's critical for parents to create a solid home base for their children. A safe and secure haven imbues children with the inner resources they need to function in the world and succeed in the classroom. But marital tension disrupts that haven and ultimately has an impact on kids' behaviors.

Dr. Harvey Karp, author of the book and DVD *The Happiest Baby on the Block,* compares parents to a team of horses. "If they go in different directions, it will make it difficult for the wagon to roll," he says.

It isn't always easy creating a home environment that nurtures a child's emotional and cognitive development. "Part of the problem is we think becoming parents shouldn't be a big deal," say John Gottman, Ph.D., and Julie Schwartz Gottman, Ph.D., in their book *And Baby Makes Three.* "But once the realities of new parenthood set in, the stresses stand out, too. Does it have to be this way? Not if we have the skills to create savory family time, instead of sour and bitter moments."

### Avoiding negative patterns

A certain amount of family tension is unavoidable. "As much as we talk of intramarriage consistency, there will always be differences and anxiety-producing situations," says clinical psychologist and author Laura Kastner, Ph.D. Those situations can escalate into patterns, unless parents or caretakers develop strategies to help themselves cope with the countless (and endless) issues parenting generates.

"Once the baby arrives, most families get into a 'dance,'" says Carolyn Pirak, a parenting expert at Talaris Institute and the former director of the national Bringing Baby Home program. "One parent steps forward, the other steps back. For some, it works.

But many people overthink the issues without allowing for flexibility."

These issues — Pirak refers to them as "hot buttons" — can range from sports (she wants the kid on the slopes by age three; he doesn't get the ski thing at all) to schools (she went to Elite Prep; he's a public-school guy) to chess club (Chess? What's wrong with basketball?).

The goal is to move from a "me" to a "we" to a "three." And that can take time. If a couple had issues before becoming parents, chances are those issues won't magically evaporate the minute they exit the birthing room. If he's always late or she's always disorganized, becoming a parent won't change that. "It's normal to disagree," Pirak says. "What you need is a strategy for disagreement."

In other words, agree to disagree, and then come up with a plan. Recognize that you enter a marriage with different goals, values, and expectations, and that you will be having lifelong discussions on these topics. Scope out your "triggers" — those annoyances that really touch a nerve — and find a way to compromise.

Susan Livingston and her husband, Tom, found ways to compromise as they raised their two daughters, now ages nine and six.

### TIPS MAKING A PLAN FOR PARENTING

- Find agreement on your core values. That's more important than agreeing on the daily tasks and challenges of parenting.
- Create a strategy for disagreement. Try to agree on a plan for discussing relationship challenges, scheduling conflicts, and parenting differences.
- Remember that you will bring your past to your parenting. By being aware of the positive and negative emotions you have about the decisions your parents made, you can make a choice to parent similarly or differently.
- Remember that children will benefit more from consistency and follow-through than from which parent's view "wins."

Source: Carolyn Pirak, parenting expert at Talaris Institute in Seattle, and former national program director of the Bringing Baby Home program

When they divorced two and a half years ago, they agreed, as Susan says, to "stay partners on the kid stuff."

Not that it's all been a breeze. They clashed over their kids' sports, over whether the girls should attend preschool, over finances.

The fix? They deal with sports one season at a time. They talked with teachers, friends, and pediatricians, and sent the girls to preschool. As for the finances . . . well, that's a work in progress.

Overall, says Susan, they've navigated the issues one at a time, with a respectable measure of success. "We know it's important to maintain a united front, and even more critical in a family where there's a divorce. Our goal is to be open and honest, and in the end, do what's best for the kids," she says. "It can work. You have to make it work."

## BECOME AN EMOTION COACH

Your baby is home! The prenatal classes, the hospital tours, the pregnancy tips from well-meaning friends — that's all behind you now. You can finally focus on Number One. That would be, in case you're wondering, the baby. There's a tiny new sheriff in town, and he's not letting you forget it. He's creating mega-noise, clamoring for spotless diapers, and gazing at you — sometimes quite intently — with those newly minted eyes.

And you're gazing right back. Not just gazing; cooing, giggling, making goofy faces, murmuring in falsetto, and pretty much acting like the silly, infant-crazed parent you never guessed you'd be.

All that cooing and smiling? It's ingrained in parents and caretakers, and happens instinctively, say child development experts. Call it bonding, call it connecting, or simply call it love; these days, it's often called "attachment." It lays the foundation for emotional well-being, which is a crucial component for learning.

Babies begin forming attachments the instant they're born. Parents, by doing what comes naturally, show their baby that his needs will be met. When the baby's wet, they change him; when he's hungry, they feed him. All those actions reinforce these attachments and equip him with the emotional tools he needs to form connections with his parents and peers.

Psychotherapist Yaffa Maritz created two successful programs — Listening Mothers and Reflective Parenting — to promote emotional bonding between parents and their babies. Maritz remembers one mother who insisted on holding her eight-month-old all the time. "She thought 'attachment' meant carrying your baby," says Maritz. But it means more than that: It means learning your baby's cues, connecting with your baby's rhythms, and understanding how he approaches the world and adapts to his environment.

**Validate your baby's feelings**

Most of us worry early on about scholastic readiness. Can our kids count? Recognize letters? Spell their names? We now know that children need more than mere academics to help them navigate their way through life. We also know that school readiness can't happen without emotional readiness. "You can't separate emotional intelligence from cognitive intelligence," says Karp. "We all know brilliant people we wouldn't want to have lunch with."

The happiest people may not always be the smartest people, but they're the ones with the best personal and social skills, says Karp. If parents pay attention to developing those kinds of skills in their children, "the cognitive stuff will just come along," he says.

How can parents help nurture their child's feelings and emotions? They can tune into them from day one. Researchers call this

**TIPS EMOTION COACHING**

- Learn your baby's cues and respond to them. Is she wet? Hungry? Tired?
- Imitate your baby's expressions and babble back when she coos and makes sounds. This helps validate her feelings.
- Help your child understand her emotions by talking about them: "I know you are sad that I'm leaving for a while, but I'll be back very soon."
- Tell her it's OK to talk about her feelings.
- Help your child find solutions for dealing with emotions such as anger or sadness.
- Teach her self-control by helping her understand which behaviors are acceptable and how the way she acts affects others.

"emotion coaching" and claim that with a little effort, mom, dad, and other caretakers can morph into first-class emotion coaches. They can start by learning to validate their baby's feelings in simple, natural ways, such as imitating facial expressions and responding to every verbal cue, coo for coo.

After eighteen months or so, they can work to develop smart coaching skills for their toddler. "Toddlers can get overwhelmed and have meltdowns," says Billie Young of the National Child Care Information and Technical Assistance Center (NCCIC), a government organization that offers child-care information and resources. "A controlling parent might say, 'Knock it off! I'm sick of that.' An emotion-coaching parent would help the child understand his behavior by saying, 'It sounds like you might be angry. It's hard to be angry, isn't it? It doesn't feel good.'"

With assistance, young children can find solutions for dealing with their anger or sadness, says Young. "You can tell a child, 'It's not OK to hit me, but you can hit the pillow.' Or, 'I know you're sad, but it's time to go to bed now. In a little bit, you're going to feel better.'"

How does helping a child cope with anger, sadness, or other feelings translate to later learning?

"It's very clear that kids who develop social and emotional capacities do better academically," says UCLA psychiatrist Dr. Daniel J. Siegel, the author of *Parenting from the Inside Out.* For example, learning the value of delayed gratification is essential for learning, Siegel says. "It also gives a child the ability to take on a challenge and realize he can rise to the occasion by trying hard at something."

Larry Macmillan, a consultant and former director of the Highline Head Start Learning Center in Seattle, targets three areas of emotional development that are linked to a child's school performance: attachment, self-control, and initiative.

"Learning takes place in the context of relationships," he says. "Attachment affects how well a child can socialize and form bonds with peers and with the teacher."

Self-control, intertwined with initiative and curiosity, is what helps a child stand in line, sit in a circle, and wait his turn.

Parents can teach self-control and initiative by helping their child understand behavior; what's acceptable and what's not. "Children possess an innate aggression to discover the world," Macmillan says. "They need to figure out ways to balance their impulses and to understand how those impulses impact others."

Kids who have trouble managing their feelings can't make friends or work in groups, Young says, and may need more time before they're ready for school. "The kindergarten teacher needs a child who talks about his feelings and deals with them in a way that doesn't make him disruptive to the class."

## TALK IT UP FOR LEARNING

Here's one of my favorite images: The big, burly, six-foot-four-inch former football player is cradling his new infant for the first time. His face softens into a wide grin as he begins to speak to his new child. His pitch? Four octaves up.

OK, four octaves might be an exaggeration. But the truth is, we all instinctively elevate our voices and draw out our vowels when speaking to a baby, though most of us couldn't say why.

We have good reason for this instinct. Parents and caretakers around the world all change their speech to make it clearer and more distinct, whether they're talking in English, Zulu, or Mandarin. We know this from research conducted by Patricia Kuhl, Ph.D., and Andrew Meltzoff, Ph.D., codirectors of the University of Washington Institute for Learning and Brain Sciences (I-LABS). Kuhl found that speaking to babies this way — she calls it "parentese" — helps them begin to understand language, a necessary skill for learning success.

Researchers are finding that the size of a child's vocabulary when he enters school directly affects his long-term success as a student.

In fact, vocabulary and oral language are better predictors of reading success than IQ, says Linda Sullivan-Dudzic, a speech and language pathologist in the Bremerton School District in Bremerton, Washington. That's because kids learn to read more easily if they've heard the words before. "It's all built on background knowledge," says Sullivan-Dudzic. The language children hear is called "receptive," and the language they speak is "expressive." The more parents talk to kids, the more words they'll develop in their receptive repertoire.

According to the Puget Sound Educational Service District's Early Literacy Outreach Project, infants who demonstrate and master the building blocks of speech at six months develop more complex language skills by ages two and three, and improve their reading abilities at four and five.

Parents should begin enriching their kids' environment with lots of language — from day one! Children absorb language long before they speak. They make "maps" and patterns of sounds they hear over and over. Kuhl's research shows that babies have "windows of opportunities" for learning sounds; if they don't hear certain sounds — say, those of a different language — by the time they're one year old, they won't be able to recognize them later.

In fact, it appears there are genuine benefits to early (really early!) foreign-language exposure. According to Kuhl's studies, babies and young children learn language differently — and better — than adults do, because there's more sensitivity to language early on. As babies begin losing that sensitivity, they begin tuning out sounds that are not relevant to the language they hear the most.

## TIPS ENCOURAGING EARLY LANGUAGE DEVELOPMENT

- Talk to your baby slowly and distinctly in a high-pitched voice, using "parentese."
- Speak to your child often from the day he's born. Sing, recite poems, and describe what you're doing during the day: "We're going in the car!" "We're going on a swing!"
- Read interactively to your child — and make it fun: "Where's the horse? That's right, there's the horse!"
- Let your child get involved while you read to him by letting him turn the pages or point to illustrations.
- Label and explain objects your young child points to: "This is a cup! We drink from a cup!"
- Don't overcorrect your child's early language attempts. That might frustrate him.

UW researchers also found that infants learn foreign language best by social interaction. In other words, watching an educational DVD or listening to an audiotape in Spanish or Cantonese doesn't really work; human contact does.

**Sing, read, and slow down**

Parents can help their children build strong vocabularies — in any language — by sharing their own excitement about words. Forget the flash cards. Just talk it up as much as you can. Sing, recite poems, read Seuss or Tolstoy — it really doesn't matter. Hold your baby close, exaggerate your words, and slow down your speech.

And read, read, read. But don't just recite words on a page; experts say the most effective approach is to read interactively. Ask your child about what he's looking at in the book. Say, "This is a cow. What does the cow say?"

With this reading technique — educators call it "dialogic reading" — the adult becomes both the questioner and the audience for the child. Rather than simply listening, the child becomes actively involved in the process. "Let your child have as much control as possible," says Mark Sabol, coordinator for Even Start, a federally funded family literacy program. "Let him turn the page or go back to another page. Have conversations about what you're reading."

Wondering what those conversations should sound like? One model is called the PEER sequence, developed by researchers at the State University of New York at Stony Brook. The PEER sequence is a simple technique that any adult can try when reading with a young child. Here are the steps:

**P**rompt the child. ("What do you see?")

**E**valuate the response. ("That's right, it's a cow.")

**E**xpand upon what the child says. ("A cow lives on a farm and says moo.")

**R**epeat the prompt to make sure the child has learned the information.

The last thing you want to do is make these sessions stressful. So whether talking, singing, or reading to your child, make it fun. That's how your child will learn to enjoy talking, reading, and, hopefully, learning.

## Q & A WITH PATRICIA KUHL, PH.D.

*Patricia Kuhl, Ph.D., is codirector at the University of Washington Institute for Learning and Brain Sciences (I-LABS) and co-author of* The Scientist in the Crib: Minds, Brains, and How Children Learn.

**Q: What kinds of sounds do infants listen to?**

Infants love to listen to people talking, especially the special language we use when we talk to babies, often called "motherese" or "parentese," because all parents use it, even those from other cultures. When given a choice between types of things to listen to, infants will choose people talking over any other auditory signal.

**Q: What is the "window of opportunity" for language acquisition?**

The data show that between zero and seven years of age, the brain is very "plastic" and has excellent language-acquisition skills. As we move toward puberty, our abilities decline systematically. It's surprising, because adults are cognitively superior to infants and young children, but the children beat us at this game. No one disputes the fact that there is a "window of opportunity" for language learning. What we're trying to figure out now is why.

**Q: How does this translate to parent-infant interaction?**

If parents want their children to be bilingual speakers, they should have their children interact in play groups with speakers of the new language. Our studies show that infants do not learn from DVD presentations or audiotapes, but through natural interactions with native speakers of another language. It's child's play when done in the right way.

**Q: What can parents do to enhance speech development?**

The most important thing parents can do is to talk to their children and let them interact in return. Adults naturally use "motherese" when talking to children, and our studies show that this style of speech is not only preferred by infants, but also is associated with advanced language development.

**Q: What are red flags, or danger signals, to look for in speech development that might indicate a problem?**

If your child does not produce first words by fourteen months or two-word combinations by twenty-two months, it's time to consult with a speech-language specialist. Hearing problems or other language problems can be diagnosed and treated early, when the brain is highly receptive to treatment. It's also important for parents to be aware if their children are not socially interested in communication — looking at the parents' faces is something that typically developing children love to do, but children with autism do not do. If parents notice that the child does not look at them, they should see a specialist.

CHAPTER 2

# Learning During the Toddler Years

## HELPING YOUR CHILD BECOME MORE SOCIAL

Anyone who's ever seen an infant coo, smile, or reach out knows it: We're social animals from day one. As the months go by, a baby's interaction increases as she looks to her parents for approval, engages them in play, and insists upon their (nearly constant) presence.

By toddlerhood, she learns something about sharing as she starts to play with other children, communicating needs and wishes.

Educators hope that by the time a child begins school, those fundamental social skills will have developed enough to enable her to take turns, cooperate, respect others, and form friendships. The goal? That by kindergarten, kids will begin learning to successfully navigate their social world — an essential skill that will help them hold their own in the classroom and throughout their lives.

"Learning to live comfortably in the company of peers is a necessary requirement for your child, a critical challenge that begins at a very early age and will continue for many years," child development expert Kenneth Rubin writes in his book *The Friendship Factor.*

In fact, social skills are directly linked to later academic success, says Jamila Reid, Ph.D., codirector of the University of Washington Parenting Clinic. "Can the child share? Recognize a peer's intentions? Listen to the teacher's instructions? Those things are as important as reading, letters, and numbers," Reid says.

### Getting along, learning to share

Parents and education policy experts often fail to recognize how crucial those social skills are and typically value academic prowess over social competence, says Reid. But child development experts agree that kids can't learn effectively unless they understand how to get along with others and function in a group.

Children are also more successful at school when they have friends. Friendships help make children feel socially validated and valued, and accepted as part of the school community — and that helps foster strong self-esteem.

Socialization has become an even bigger player in the schoolhouse, as more teachers focus on "collaborative learning." These days, young students routinely study and exchange ideas in group settings or circles. Teachers arrange tables and desks in clusters to foster discussions, group interaction, and a cooperative environment.

Parents can help boost collaborative learning by discussing what it means to "play fair" and by talking about playground rules, such as sometimes letting others go first. "You can model sharing," Reid says. "Say, 'I'm going to share this block with you. Isn't that great? You just shared that with me!'"

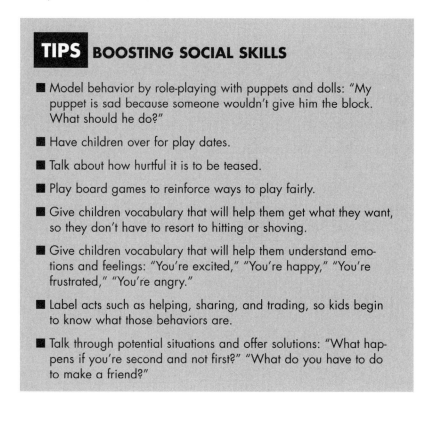

## TIPS BOOSTING SOCIAL SKILLS

- Model behavior by role-playing with puppets and dolls: "My puppet is sad because someone wouldn't give him the block. What should he do?"
- Have children over for play dates.
- Talk about how hurtful it is to be teased.
- Play board games to reinforce ways to play fairly.
- Give children vocabulary that will help them get what they want, so they don't have to resort to hitting or shoving.
- Give children vocabulary that will help them understand emotions and feelings: "You're excited," "You're happy," "You're frustrated," "You're angry."
- Label acts such as helping, sharing, and trading, so kids begin to know what those behaviors are.
- Talk through potential situations and offer solutions: "What happens if you're second and not first?" "What do you have to do to make a friend?"

## KEEP 'EM MOVING

We know that kids love to move; that's why we enroll them in T-ball, cart them to parks, and watch them at mini-gyms. We enjoy the exuberance, energy, and sheer delight they exhibit as they climb, somersault, and prance through the maze of whatever activity is at hand.

What parents may not realize is that when kids move their bodies, nerve cells in their brains are getting crucial stimulation. "Movement creates neural activity and connections that literally grow the brain," says Helene Freda, an education specialist who is now senior program developer for the international company Gymboree Play and Music. "When it's combined with other sensory experiences, movement is the foundation for all learning."

That's why some of the most valuable early childhood experiences are those that keep kids moving — and that also involve touch, sight, and sound.

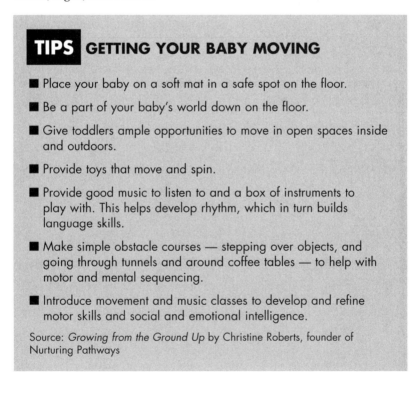

### TIPS GETTING YOUR BABY MOVING

- Place your baby on a soft mat in a safe spot on the floor.
- Be a part of your baby's world down on the floor.
- Give toddlers ample opportunities to move in open spaces inside and outdoors.
- Provide toys that move and spin.
- Provide good music to listen to and a box of instruments to play with. This helps develop rhythm, which in turn builds language skills.
- Make simple obstacle courses — stepping over objects, and going through tunnels and around coffee tables — to help with motor and mental sequencing.
- Introduce movement and music classes to develop and refine motor skills and social and emotional intelligence.

Source: *Growing from the Ground Up* by Christine Roberts, founder of Nurturing Pathways

### Floor play

Christine Roberts is a big believer in what she calls "floor play." Roberts developed Nurturing Pathways, a Seattle-area early childhood creative dance program for kids from newborn through age three. She believes in keeping young children out of bouncers and seats. Instead, she says, let them play on the floor and give them plenty of opportunity to move and explore.

That means less TV, video, and computer time, and more whole-body movement — which sometimes translates into just plain playing. "The less we move, the less we use our neural networks," says Roberts. "If we're using our whole body, we are engaging more parts of our whole brain. And for a developing brain, that's very significant."

When Robin Wes founded The Little Gym 30 years ago, he worked to create a program that would help children hone their motor skills while also developing their emotional, social, and cognitive abilities. Since those early days, The Little Gym has expanded to more than 300 franchises around the world.

In movement, tumbling, yoga, and other action-packed classes such as those offered by Gymboree and The Little Gym, toddlers and preschoolers learn to follow directions, listen, take risks, solve problems, and focus. They learn more about their bodies ("Hold your hands up!"), about direction ("Turn around!"), and even about rhythm ("Clap your hands to the music!").

"While a preschooler explores, he looks at a situation and sizes it up," says Wes. "He might ask himself, 'What could I do on that balance beam?' Then he has to make a decision. This builds readiness proficiency for that first day of kindergarten."

## Q & A WITH ROBIN WES

*Robin Wes is founder of The Little Gym International, Inc.*

**Q: Do exercise and movement translate into learning and education?**

According to several studies, yes. Scientists have discovered that three-year-olds with more highly developed motor skills show a greater level of school readiness and perform better in kindergarten than those with less developed motor skills.

**Q: In what ways have you seen kids evolve physically and cognitively through this kind of play?**

At The Little Gym, you notice that the children who start very young — at age four months — are more comfortable in the group, follow directions more easily, and are socially and emotionally more developed compared to three-year-olds just beginning a non-parent participation class. Generally, their language skills are better and their motor-skill development is more mature.

**Q: What additional skills do children learn in gym and other movement classes?**

They learn readiness skills for the first day of kindergarten, such as listening skills, social skills, motor skills, and language skills, and they learn to follow directions.

**Q: Are there other ways parents can encourage these kinds of activities at home?**

Get kids active by being a good model. Never ask your kids to do what you won't do yourself. Engage in physical activities: Go biking or swimming and play outside. Big toys and forts will keep kids busy for hours.

Take away the competitive angle and do not judge the performance. All too often, if parents take a child swimming, they become the teacher, and the fun factor is reduced. Do not coach from the side; it sends "not good enough" messages to your children. Have realistic expectations of your child's developmental stage.

**Q: How does "getting physical" promote emotional intelligence?**

Educators are finding that kids who can handle the emotions that come up in daily life are healthier and do better at school. Participation in a gym class creates many opportunities for kids of all ages to learn the language of emotions. If a two-year-old grabs another two-year-old's ball, and the parents use that opportunity to teach the correct behavior (as opposed to hitting or shoving), then the language of the emotional world is learned.

**Q: How do movement classes help kids learn to take risks?**

Let's say a three-year-old is afraid to come into class. Having a compassionate parent's support helps the child overcome that fear. Taking risks is a big part of learning and an essential behavior a child must master in order to be able to learn. Participation in a gym class reinforces risk taking, perseverance, the ability to handle failure, and the power of success.

## MAKING LEARNING CHILD-CENTERED

Think back to your second-grade classroom. Chances are, your experience was more Ferris Bueller than Summerhill School. You sat at your desk and tried to stay attentive while your teacher droned on (and on) about places and dates you didn't remember two weeks later.

But now (finally!) educators realize that kids don't actually learn that way. That's why fewer and fewer schools are using the traditional sit-and-listen approach. The teaching method that's grown in acceptance and popularity over the last decade is called "child-centered learning." It's a technique — and a philosophy of education — that focuses on the student, not the teacher or a set curriculum. Child-centered learning highlights collaboration: Instructors, child-care providers, and parents take their cues from the kids, drawing upon their interests, needs, and natural curiosity.

Early learning experts encourage parents to think about settings that are child-centered when shopping for preschools and kindergartens, and when interacting with their own young children. "Child-centered learning is huge for school readiness," says Bridgett Chandler, director of public affairs with Seattle Public Schools. "It means the child has had adults saying to him, 'I know you are a learner. I trust you as someone who has good ideas.'"

Here's how child-centered learning can work in the classroom: A group of three-year-olds is chatting about the word "power." What is power? Who has it? That conversation — which actually happened in Chandler's daughter's class — then leads to a month-long exploration of the concept of power. The children paint and talk about what happens when they draw one color on top of another. Red, they find, is stronger than yellow. Then the teacher places a glob of clay in front of them. If paint has power, do other things have power, too?

"Most of the time, when people think about teaching kids, it's about what they want the children to know," Chandler says.

"When instruction is child-centered, the child is trusted as someone who is capable of having his or her own ideas about how the world works. The teacher is there to interact, based on what the child shows her is important, interesting, and delightful."

Is it effective? Diane Kroll thinks so. Kroll is director of Puget Sound Education Service District (PSESD), an early childhood educational service agency. "When you're doing something that engages you, you are more likely to remember it and want to do more," she says, and that's how it works for youngsters. "When children are able to explore and be involved, they will hold on to that information," Kroll says. "It sticks."

### Developing a love of learning

Children develop self-confidence and begin to trust their own capabilities when they play a role in their own education, Kroll says. "A child-centered environment creates a love of knowledge. In it, children feel competent, capable, and ready to learn."

Child-centered learning can begin early, says early childhood instructor Susan Hakoda. "Infants aren't verbal, but they communicate in other ways," she says. "It's up to adults to pick up on their cues."

Is your toddler losing interest in a story? Switch gears. The key is to stay in tune and in touch with your child's interests and needs — and to know when to throw in an extra prop or toy.

Enriching children's environments this way can have an impact on social and emotional growth. "When it's all about them, it makes them feel good," says Hakoda. Often, adults get in the way

**TIPS CHILD-CENTERED LEARNING**

- Pay attention to your child and learn to react to his cues.
- Avoid testing, quizzing, and drilling your child.
- Keep questions open-ended.
- Instead of teaching your child numbers, give him objects to count.
- Look for preschools and kindergartens that are child-centered.

of making learning fun. "We think testing and drilling is the way children learn, because that's how we were taught," Hakoda says. "But they'll learn just as well if we just talk to them about shapes and numbers. It's not about teaching them math at age two; it's about giving them experiences with things they can count."

The best instructors — whether teachers or parents — offer children a wide range of experiences, Hakoda says. "Explain what you are doing and what you see the child doing." Keep questions open-ended and stay away from rote testing; it's a turn-off. "Instead of asking, 'What color is the ball?' ask, 'Can you pass me the red ball?' Don't be your child's teacher, be his guide."

## THE POWER OF THE ARTS

How important are the arts? They're right up there with vocabulary and literacy, claim educators, who advise parents to get kids involved in art activities early. Researchers say there's reason to believe music stimulates your infant's brain, dance helps develop motor skills, and drama teaches emotions and problem-solving skills.

And that's just the beginning. Years ago, the U.S. Department of Education reported that preschoolers who were given keyboard lessons and participated in group singing scored higher on spatial reasoning tests.[1] Such information is rarely ignored by ever-alert toy executives. In fact, it's why formerly silent objects — such as dollhouses — now broadcast Pachelbel's Canon while stimulating your child's other sensory receptors with flashing lights and fuzzy objects. It's also the reason why there are more early-learning music, art, and drama programs out there than ever — with a plethora of books, CDs, and DVDs to accompany them.

While experts and educators agree that some parents take the theory too far (you'd probably enjoy Chopin more than your six-week-old would), they also report that music, painting, storytelling, and acting can indeed help children learn.

"The arts are a thinking tool, a way for children to communicate understanding and misunderstandings, and confront them," says Margie Carter, an early childhood specialist and co-author of

[1] National Education Longitudinal Study (NELS: 88), *U.S. Department of Education Bulletin* (Washington, D.C.: 1988).

*Training Teachers: A Harvest of Theory and Practice.* "If you turn an idea into a drawing or sculpture, you can figure out things you'd never figure out if you just tried to explain. The purpose of the arts goes way beyond creativity and imagination."

The arts play an important role in getting your kids ready for kindergarten, says Rachel Glass, a Seattle-area drama, music, and dance teacher. "School is so much more than reading, writing, and arithmetic," Glass says. "The arts provide a way for children to discover they can make a contribution; it empowers them and raises their self-esteem. The arts let children put their own individual stamp on what they are good at."

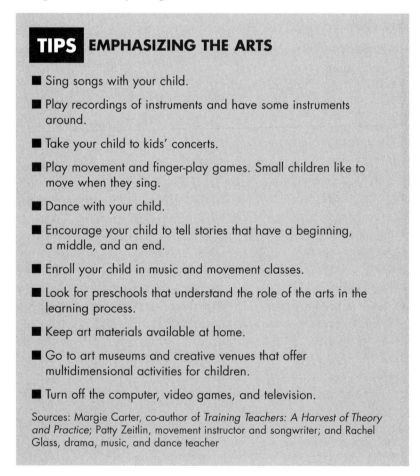

### TIPS EMPHASIZING THE ARTS

- Sing songs with your child.
- Play recordings of instruments and have some instruments around.
- Take your child to kids' concerts.
- Play movement and finger-play games. Small children like to move when they sing.
- Dance with your child.
- Encourage your child to tell stories that have a beginning, a middle, and an end.
- Enroll your child in music and movement classes.
- Look for preschools that understand the role of the arts in the learning process.
- Keep art materials available at home.
- Go to art museums and creative venues that offer multidimensional activities for children.
- Turn off the computer, video games, and television.

Sources: Margie Carter, co-author of *Training Teachers: A Harvest of Theory and Practice;* Patty Zeitlin, movement instructor and songwriter; and Rachel Glass, drama, music, and dance teacher

**Drawing, acting, and music**

The arts help broaden children's abilities in other ways. Drawing, for example, can address emotional development. "What does a happy face look like? A mad face? Children can draw and describe it," says Glass. "This is a way for them to understand what makes them happy, sad, or afraid."

Acting can help children learn more about empathy and other emotions, as they watch kids express them through drama games and role-playing. These games also offer kids alternative ways to work through problems and deal with frustrations, Glass says. "They act out what it's like to be angry or afraid. They learn, 'What can I do to help myself when I'm mad or when I'm sad?'"

Drama and storytelling can help increase your child's vocabulary. Let's say another three-year-old gets up and pretends she's a lion. Your child might comment, "She was showing her teeth! She was roaring!"

Acting also helps kids develop organization and memory skills, Glass says. "A child who is performing must remember what his part is and what comes next."

The benefits of music earned particular buzz after researchers identified the "Mozart Effect" more than 10 years ago and suggested that listening to 10 minutes of Mozart before a spatial-skills test improved performance. While the actual relationship between music and IQ remains unclear, music and movement instructor Patty Zeitlin feels that music can enhance cognitive skills. Zeitlin has recorded seven albums of original songs for children and is the author of *A Song Is a Rainbow*, a textbook for preschool and kindergarten teachers. "The more you use language — talking or singing — the richer the brain connections are. The long, drawn-out vowels of singing nourish brain development," she says.

Music also serves as a language and learning vehicle for preverbal children, Zeitlin says. "Babies respond naturally to music by moving and vocalizing. Later on, they can create their own words to songs. This stimulates creativity and cognitive development."

## Q & A WITH LINDA HARTZELL

*Linda Hartzell is artistic director of the Seattle Children's Theatre and its education programs.*

**Q: How can music and drama enrich a child's environment?**

Music and drama are part of the human experience and part of who we are as human beings. Both music and drama are basic to life; storytelling, for example, is the most basic of human experiences, and humming a song is natural. Just as we smile, listen, and talk, singing and telling stories and using your imagination to see the world is part of life. The arts help children hone their perceptive and imaginative skills, and enhance their ability to create their own world.

**Q: What kinds of skills do children glean from acting and music participation?**

Acting utilizes the whole body and helps children develop listening skills. They use their ears and eyes to hear and read music, and their motor skills to play an instrument. Acting requires movement, which also helps develop motor skills.

Both music and drama teach kids how to take risks. They must play or perform in front of many people. They learn to stick to it, to play it out. There's always a goal to execute. Through drive and focus, these kids persevere. And those are qualities they can take with them throughout their lives.

Most of all, through activities such as drama and music, children become more observant and aware of the world around them. In that process, they evolve into more socialized and perceptive human beings.

**Q: How does acting and imaginary play help young children develop emotionally?**

Much like athletics, acting requires "team" participation. There's a give-and-take that also happens in sports.

Acting also requires actors to understand a story from another point of view. To develop a character, you must develop empathy. Through the story and the character, you learn about cause and effect, and that there's a moral reaction to good, bad, sad, and happy. These kinds of experiences help children have a better sense of emotions, including their own.

**Q: In what other ways do art, music, and drama affect and shape kids?**

Involvement in the arts involves the whole child. It helps them learn to interact with others and can really develop self-esteem. I taught drama and directed plays and musicals at Lakeside School in Seattle for 17 years. That's why I understand *High School Musical* — I lived it. I know that every child becomes a part of the process. Students learn that the group is more important than the individual. The theater experience provides a community for these kids and breaks down clique barriers.

Music and art are the things that make us feel, that go to the inner soul. It gives kids a sense of purpose. Doesn't every child need to feel a measure of success? Just finishing a play . . . that imparts a sense of success.

**Q: What can parents do to inject the arts — and an appreciation for them — into their children's lives?**

Provide a space and a time for creative play. Let your children use their minds and bodies in their play — and leave room for interpretation. In other words, don't try to connect all the dots. You want your children to develop their own world of possibilities.

Come up with opportunities for pretend and imaginative play — and be a participant. Play, pretend, and sing with your kids.

Enroll them in drama and music classes; these activities should be part of their everyday lives, as it is in other cultures.

Frequent arts events with your children. Take them to plays and to music and dance performances, and support the arts.

## HOW TO FIND A PRESCHOOL

If you went to preschool as a child, you probably loved it. Back then, preschool meant puzzles, paints, and plenty of play. Kids adored playing "musical chairs," were crazy for crackers, and at rest time, dutifully rolled out blankets and teddy bears.

I have no idea whether Miss Mimi — my own practically perfect preschool teacher — followed any sort of standardized curriculum. I do remember missing song time to work on a "family portrait." I also remember feeling happy and secure in that class, while somehow managing to meet the requisite scholastic objectives, which in those days amounted to "gets along well with others."

Simplicity is bliss. But then, so, as they say, is ignorance. Maybe that's why navigating the preschool terrain these days is considerably more complicated. The truth is, we know more than we used to. Thanks to advances in child development and neuroscience, parents and educators are paying closer attention to the way kids process information during those prekindergarten years.

We know, for example, that early socialization facilitates learning. And that while you can provide your children with countless opportunities for social interaction at home, the kind of group context kids encounter in a school setting is difficult to duplicate.

Take "circle time." It gives kids a chance to begin mastering concepts such as sharing, taking turns, and respecting one another. Learning to give and take promotes emotional values such as empathy and compassion, essential qualities for your child's overall emotional health and development.

We know that while all play promotes learning, physical play helps children develop physical and cognitive skills, and creative play helps them connect with their own feelings. And we realize that early childhood education experts — using carefully selected games and materials most of us don't stash in the playroom — understand how to maximize that play environment.

### What to look for

Early education programs have proliferated over the last few decades, so much so that the array of philosophies and preschool options available today can be downright confusing. What'll it be: Montessori? Reggio Emilia? Waldorf? The days when parents happily "settled" for the little nursery school down the block seem a distant memory.

Though programs vary, the kinds of elements that shape excellent preschools remain consistent, experts say. So before stressing over educational theories and learning philosophies, take a look at the big picture: Think about what kind of environment you'd like — overall — for your child.

For starters, look for quality, says Jerlean Daniel, Ph.D., deputy executive director of the National Association for the Education of Young Children (NAEYC). "Good preschools give children a readiness boost for the rest of their lives," says Daniel. "When a program is very high in quality, you get excellent results."

How do you identify a quality preschool?

Check out the teachers. Are they qualified? NAEYC professionals feel preschool teachers should hold degrees in early childhood education. "This tells parents these are people who have studied children and have studied education," says Daniel.

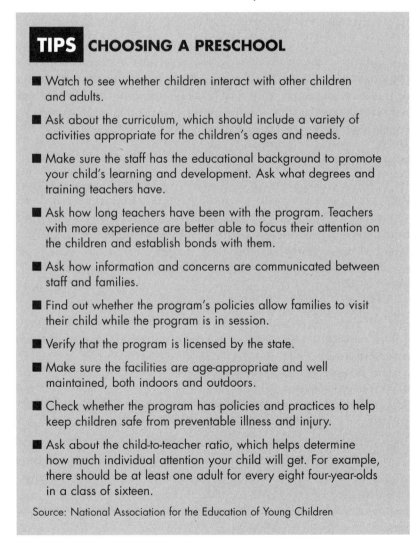

## TIPS CHOOSING A PRESCHOOL

- Watch to see whether children interact with other children and adults.
- Ask about the curriculum, which should include a variety of activities appropriate for the children's ages and needs.
- Make sure the staff has the educational background to promote your child's learning and development. Ask what degrees and training teachers have.
- Ask how long teachers have been with the program. Teachers with more experience are better able to focus their attention on the children and establish bonds with them.
- Ask how information and concerns are communicated between staff and families.
- Find out whether the program's policies allow families to visit their child while the program is in session.
- Verify that the program is licensed by the state.
- Make sure the facilities are age-appropriate and well maintained, both indoors and outdoors.
- Check whether the program has policies and practices to help keep children safe from preventable illness and injury.
- Ask about the child-to-teacher ratio, which helps determine how much individual attention your child will get. For example, there should be at least one adult for every eight four-year-olds in a class of sixteen.

Source: National Association for the Education of Young Children

Find out if those teachers stick around. Frequent staff turnover undermines stability. "Young children learn at their best when they have consistent relationships with the adults in the program," says Daniel. "A big turnover means constant shifting and makes it more difficult for kids to build those connections."

Quality early learning experiences come in many shapes and sizes, says Marty Jacobs, family services director at Child Care Resources, a Seattle-area nonprofit referral agency. "Parents must make sure their own values are consistent with the program they select."

So look for a program that fits your child and jells with your own cultural background and worldview. What's your youngster's personality like? Would he be happier in a busy, boisterous setting or in a more subdued, quiet one? Ask about discipline policies and behavioral expectations, and make sure you and any school you're considering share similar beliefs.

**What's your style?**

Next, find out how kids spend their day at different preschools. Do they play outdoors? Work on computers? Take field trips? In Montessori classrooms, everything has a purpose, and you won't find dress-up corners, for example. But you might see them in a Waldorf program, where cooking, singing, art, story time, and dress-up thrive. "We find children learn most efficiently through play," says Meg Petty, admissions director at the Seattle Waldorf School. "Materials — such as driftwood, stones, chestnuts, and seashells — come from nature. Natural materials engage the senses. And by manipulating these toys, the children are engaging their imaginations."

The Reggio Emilia approach emphasizes collaboration; groups work together, with teachers taking their cues from the kids. "We listen to the children and investigate what they are interested in," says PSESD's Kroll. "We see the child as competent, capable, and ready to learn; we see the teacher as the researcher."

Maybe a cooperative preschool is more your style; these are run by parent volunteers and often less expensive than other programs. If spirituality is important to you, check out your church, synagogue, or temple; many offer preschool programs. Some of these programs welcome children of diverse religious backgrounds.

Visit a variety of schools and watch the way the adults interact with the children. "Look for teachers who are interested, engaged, and enthusiastic, who like the children and like being there," says Jacobs.

Kroll says teaching should be "intentional." That means teachers should have a plan. "They should know why they are doing what they are doing, and what they are trying to accomplish," she says.

Examine the classroom and determine if it's clean and organized. "The environment should invite children to explore," says Kroll.

Then take a good, close look at the kids. Are they happy? Having fun? Engrossed in activities? "Get a feel for the tenor and tempo of the class," says Daniel. "Go there when things are happening. Then ask yourself, can I imagine my child in that room?"

Other things to consider: Is the school accredited by the NAEYC? The NAEYC sets standards preschools must meet to earn accreditation. You can check the association's Web site (*naeyc.org*) to learn more. While you're at it, find out if the program is licensed by your state.

Check out teacher-child ratios. Current NAEYC standards require one teacher per six students in a class of twelve two-and-a-half- to three-year-olds, for example. At age four, the ratio should be one teacher for eight students in a class of sixteen. Go to the NAEYC Web site for teacher-child ratio charts.

Finally, consider cost (this can vary widely), location (do you need a program that's close to your home or to your office?), and schedule. Working parents might need full-time before- and after-school care. Others may opt to send their tots to school for a few hours a day, several times a week.

CHAPTER 3

# Getting Kindergarten Ready

## IS HE REALLY READY?

The question "When should my child begin kindergarten?" once had a simple answer: When he's old enough to go.

Oh, for the good old days. It's been decades since parents — on blissful autopilot — checked out the school eligibility date, packed up the Lone Ranger lunch box, and sent Johnny on his way.

Today, most parents take a close, careful look at their child before signing him or her up for kindergarten at the age-appropriate time. Some decide — for a range of reasons — that their five-year-old is not quite ready for school and could benefit from spending another year in preschool or at home.

Kids with summer and early fall birthdays — close to state cut-off dates — present particular dilemmas: Will they be the youngest in the class? Will they be less mature, socialized, or academically prepared than their peers? Will they be smaller and less competitive in sports?

Parents seem particularly worried about their sons, who often lag behind girls in motor and language skills. Although boys eventually catch up, some parents and educators feel postponing kindergarten for a year enables boys to compete on a more even playing field — or even enjoy a bit of an edge.

What's more, kindergarten is not the romp in the sandbox it used to be, a fact that's raised the parental anxiety level to new heights. A push for more academics and standardized testing has translated into revamped, upgraded kindergarten programs, making today's kindergarten classes look much more like yesterday's first grade.

But keeping kids back — experts call it "academic redshirting" — also has its downsides. According to a study published in the late 1990s in *Pediatrics,* the journal of the American Academy of Pediatrics, the number of kids — ages six to eight — who were

**TIPS** **ASSESSING WHEN TO START KINDERGARTEN**

- Make sure your child fits in with his peers. If he seems to fit in better with a younger group, think twice before sending him.
- Pay attention to your child's willingness to share and ability to sit still. Is he antsy? Can he focus on one activity at a time?
- Look closely at your child's learning style. Making a good match — the school, the teacher, the class — is a more important consideration than chronological age.
- If you suspect your child has a learning disability, get him into the classroom. School may be where your child can get the help he needs.

older than their same-grade peers doubled from 11 percent in 1971 to 22 percent in 1990.

Call it the Aging of Kindergarten.

"Holding a child out of kindergarten to get the physical maturity advantage has thrown everything off kilter and resulted in there being two or more years difference in ages in the same grade," says Carol Robins, a Seattle-area counselor and educational consultant. "As a consequence, a disproportionate number of kids look a head taller than others — and behave in unexpected ways, developmentally and socially." The older kids, she says, often become either leaders or bullies, and the younger ones end up being left out — or becoming followers.

So how do parents make that thorny send-them-or-hold-them decision?

Know your own child, Robins advises. "Each child and family differ, as do the economic and cultural contexts in which children grow up," she says. She suggests parents interview preschool teachers, friends, and educational consultants to gather a more objective assessment of their child.

Investigate programs appropriate to your child's needs and learning style. Ask yourself what kinds of expectations you have of your child. What are you looking for in a school?

Most importantly, evaluate your child's emotional and social readiness. Sometimes, it all comes down to maturity, educators say.

## READY, SET, GO!

You've made your decision; kindergarten starts soon. What can you do now to boost your child's readiness?

"Readiness" is a sweeping concept that's defined any number of ways. Covering everything from emotional development to cognitive skills, it can mean learning to cope, pay attention, and get along with others — or learning to count, put on a jacket, and recognize colors.

The experts claim the real readiness process begins at birth, not on kindergarten sign-up day. But as that day nears, it's helpful to store some concrete preparation skills in your box of parenting tools.

For example, remember those social skills you've been helping your child develop? They really start to count as that first day of school draws near. Now you can start building on the social abilities your child has already mastered by exposing her to more settings — the museum, the library, the zoo — where she can interact with other kids.

Learning to deal with others — and get along with them — is an important kindergarten skill. Kids need to respect the rights (and the differences) of the children they are about to spend many hours with in class. So talk to your kids about how to treat others, suggests Julia Matthews, kindergarten transition coordinator for Seattle Public Schools. Come up with ideas for solving problems and techniques your child can use to resolve conflicts without resorting to fighting. "Ask them what solutions they can think of," she says. "If they can't offer suggestions, you can."

Work with your child to develop a longer attention span. That's a critical readiness skill kids can master with a little help from parents or caretakers. Educators suggest replicating "circle time" by gathering at home and singing, reading, or talking. Help your child learn to sit still and "go with the flow" in a group setting, and try to get your child to focus on an activity for more than 10 or 15 minutes.

### Come with a few skills

Coming to kindergarten with a few basic skills can help, says Matthews. "Some preschools don't have a set curriculum, but operate more like all-day playtime sessions," she says. "It's sometimes up to parents to introduce concepts like colors and numbers."

Thanks to increasing expectations at the elementary and secondary levels, and to legislation such as the No Child Left Behind Act, the learning bar has been raised. Counting to ten, naming primary colors, and recognizing the letters of the alphabet are all good to know before entering kindergarten, according to Matthews and an increasing number of educators.

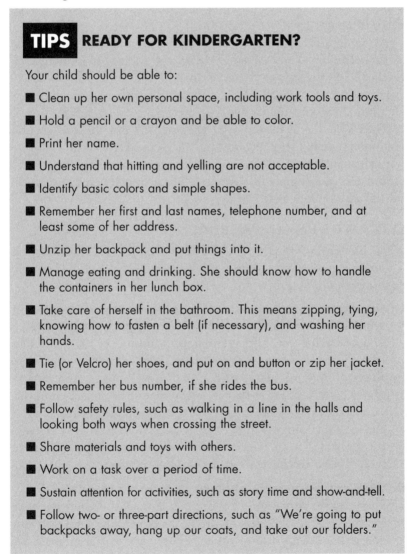

### TIPS READY FOR KINDERGARTEN?

Your child should be able to:

- Clean up her own personal space, including work tools and toys.
- Hold a pencil or a crayon and be able to color.
- Print her name.
- Understand that hitting and yelling are not acceptable.
- Identify basic colors and simple shapes.
- Remember her first and last names, telephone number, and at least some of her address.
- Unzip her backpack and put things into it.
- Manage eating and drinking. She should know how to handle the containers in her lunch box.
- Take care of herself in the bathroom. This means zipping, tying, knowing how to fasten a belt (if necessary), and washing her hands.
- Tie (or Velcro) her shoes, and put on and button or zip her jacket.
- Remember her bus number, if she rides the bus.
- Follow safety rules, such as walking in a line in the halls and looking both ways when crossing the street.
- Share materials and toys with others.
- Work on a task over a period of time.
- Sustain attention for activities, such as story time and show-and-tell.
- Follow two- or three-part directions, such as "We're going to put backpacks away, hang up our coats, and take out our folders."

Exposing children to books, words, and experiences will help establish them as lifelong learners. "Talk and listen," says Linda Averill, Ph.D., principal at Shoreline Children's Center near Seattle. "Do that in the supermarket and in your living room. Read to your kids and use libraries." Kids who have acquired sizable vocabularies in their early years come to kindergarten better equipped, she says. "Many students who enter school with vocabulary deficits never catch up."

As the first day nears, start playing the "school" game with them at dinnertime, suggests Diana Miller, a Seattle-area kindergarten teacher. "Tell the kids to raise their hand — and then call on them," she says. Reenact typical school traditions, which might include circle time, show-and-tell, and taking turns.

Then visit the school and let the kids try out the playground equipment. Help them become familiar — and more comfortable — with their new surroundings. And let them know that you think school and learning are important. "Tell them it's their job to go to school and do their best," Miller says.

## Q & A WITH NINA AUERBACH

*Nina Auerbach is president and CEO of Thrive by Five Washington, a public-private partnership that promotes positive early-learning opportunities for children, from birth to age five.*

**Q: Has the increased emphasis on academics in schools affected what kids need to know before entering kindergarten?**

One of the biggest shifts in public education over the past ten to fifteen years is the expectation that public schools must educate all children — not just *some* children — well. And schools know that if children start with a solid foundation of social, emotional, and cognitive skills, many, many more children have a better chance of doing well throughout school and graduating. Research clearly shows that children who start school behind in their skills often have a very hard time catching up.

**Q: What can parents do at home to promote these skills?**

Share books with your children; talk to your children; take advantage of all opportunities to help your children develop language. Also, exposure to other children and social interactions are important for helping children get ready for classroom settings. Helping children understand and put words to feelings, to share and get along with other kids, and building their self-esteem are all very important in raising emotionally intelligent children. Examples of "all opportunities" include counting fruit at the grocery store or spelling out stop signs while in the car.

**Q: Should parents be concerned about emotional readiness and maturity?**
Yes. When kindergarten teachers [in Washington state] were surveyed in 2005 about children's readiness for school, not only did they estimate that fewer than half were fully prepared, but they also said the biggest deficit was social-emotional development. For example, children were having trouble managing their emotions and getting along with others.

**Q: What can parents do to help their children become socially ready for kindergarten?**
Parents can make a big difference by having a good bond with their child. With a solid bond in place, a child is better able to have good relationships with others. Parents also should be continually talking with their child about feelings, empathy for other children, and sharing. Modeling good social behavior and talking about it is very helpful. Group activities like preschool and play groups — formal or informal — also help. Being able to make friends is a critical piece of being socially ready in general.

**Q: How can parents tell if their child is ready for kindergarten?**
Parents know their child better than anyone else and will be able to see their development and gauge their preparedness. Some children may be ready for kindergarten even if they only turned five over the summer, while others could benefit from waiting another year.

Most kindergarten teachers will tell you that having children socially ready for kindergarten is just as important, if not more important, than knowing their ABCs and 1-2-3s. Children need to be able to get along with other children, sit still, follow directions, and pay attention — all the things that are necessary in a classroom situation — at least for brief periods of time. Again, this is why it is so critical for parents to get their child into social activities with peers as early as possible. Also, it's helpful to visit the school before the child starts, maybe even multiple times.

**Q: Why is it important to be "kindergarten ready"?**

School demands a great deal of children, both cognitively and in terms of social and emotional maturity. It doesn't matter how "smart" a child is if they can't get along with other kids, listen to the teacher, or sit still. Being successful in school and in life has to do with both emotional and cognitive skills. The more "ready" the child is in both realms, the more likely they will be able to successfully navigate the school experience, learn what they need to learn to perform academically, and get along in the classroom setting.

But let's remember that it's not just up to the kids. Parents, teachers, and schools must be "ready" as well. The best thing for a parent to do is become a partner in their child's education. Get to know your child's teacher, introduce yourself to other parents, and get involved in volunteer programs at school. Being involved as a parent is a critical factor to your child's overall success.

## MAKING THE TRANSITION WORK

Your child is about to embark upon what promises to be the great adventure of his young life: kindergarten.

Every parent hopes the transition into kindergarten will be a smooth one. Kindergarten, after all, is a child's introduction to formal schooling and all the opportunities, expectations, and dreams that go along with it. For many kids, it's also a first bid for independence.

That's why it's disappointing — even upsetting — when your child enters the classroom that first day with the weight of the world, along with his Spiderman backpack, upon those small shoulders. We've all seen the kids who tearfully cling to their moms, dads, or caretakers those first few days.

Even children who have spent time in day cares and preschools can find kindergarten a scary experience, says Kathy Gildea, a Seattle-area elementary school counselor. "Kids encounter more responsibility in kindergarten, such as learning to follow rules in the classroom and acclimating to a structured schedule," she says.

"There's often a cafeteria, recess, music class, and a whole new group of kids engaging in activities. There's a lot that happens."

One way for parents to help their young student deal with these fears is to start mastering their own. Children sense anxiety and can often tell if their parents feel stressed about the school, the separation, or the goodbye at the school door. Teachers suggest parents set a positive tone and do not (do not!) hang around the classroom after dropping off their children.

Diane Zipperman, a counselor at the Jewish Day School of Greater Seattle, says visiting the school with your child — before that first day — is an effective way to help diffuse a child's kindergarten angst.

What else can parents do? Over the summer, look for opportunities to make references to school. "Point out the back-to-school sales or shows on TV and say things like, 'When you go to school, this is what you'll be doing,'" Zipperman says.

When talking to your kids about school, pay attention to their reactions. Do they have mistaken ideas? Have they heard frightening tales? "Now's the time for parents to have private conversations with older siblings," Zipperman says. "Tell them to save the horror stories about that incident on the playground."

## TIPS EASING THE TRANSITION TO KINDERGARTEN

- Address your own feelings. Are you anxious about your child starting kindergarten? Set a positive tone.
- If possible, visit the school in advance.
- Talk to your child. Root out rumors and frightening school stories.
- Take fun school-related outings with your child (such as shopping for school supplies).
- Introduce school routines ahead of time, such as getting clothes ready the night before.
- Reassure your child he'll be fine.
- Make a quick exit at the school or classroom door.

Introduce rituals, such as shopping for school clothes and selecting a lunchbox, letting children participate. This makes going to school more of a reality.

The week before kindergarten begins, establish routines, such as waking up at a specific time each morning and getting school clothes ready, she advises. And when that first day arrives, stay calm and matter of fact.

"This is an experience that is exciting but also bittersweet," she says. "For parents, it can evoke emotions, such as sadness or ambivalence. It's important that we recognize our own mixed feelings; they are normal and natural to have, both for parents and for children."

If the child does have trouble separating, reassure him. Tell him he'll be all right — and then make a quick exit.

"Teachers are skilled at steering these kids toward an activity; most of them calm down," Zipperman notes. "The majority of children make a good transition."

## HELPING YOUR CHILD EAT RIGHT AT SCHOOL

Once you and your child settle into a comfortable school routine, you can begin fine-tuning some daily basics. For starters: What do you put in your child's lunch box?

The government's latest dietary guidelines make the old ones look like, well, child's play. While the guidelines can be scaled down for kids, the message stays the same: more whole grains, fruits, and vegetables; less meat, bread, and pasta. That means sending your youngster off to school fueled with a bowl of Rice Krispies and toting a bag filled with bagels, chips, and juice won't cut it.

What's a parent to do?

For starters, don't worry, advises Goldie Caughlan, nutrition education manager at PCC Natural Markets in Seattle. "Have a positive attitude toward food," Caughlan says. "Model eating it yourselves and keep offering nutritious food in new presentations."

There's plenty of talk these days about childhood obesity. But it's not only obesity that's at stake when children's nutritional needs aren't being met. Experts claim well-nourished kids learn better in school. According to the national nonprofit advocacy group Action for Healthy Kids, even moderate undernutrition can have lasting

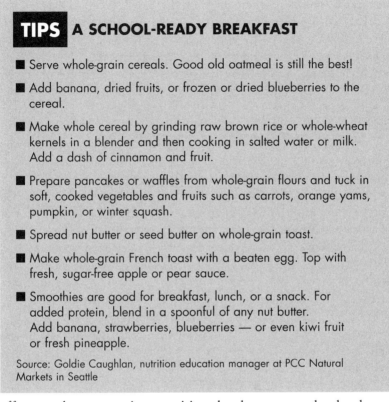

**TIPS** **A SCHOOL-READY BREAKFAST**

- Serve whole-grain cereals. Good old oatmeal is still the best!
- Add banana, dried fruits, or frozen or dried blueberries to the cereal.
- Make whole cereal by grinding raw brown rice or whole-wheat kernels in a blender and then cooking in salted water or milk. Add a dash of cinnamon and fruit.
- Prepare pancakes or waffles from whole-grain flours and tuck in soft, cooked vegetables and fruits such as carrots, orange yams, pumpkin, or winter squash.
- Spread nut butter or seed butter on whole-grain toast.
- Make whole-grain French toast with a beaten egg. Top with fresh, sugar-free apple or pear sauce.
- Smoothies are good for breakfast, lunch, or a snack. For added protein, blend in a spoonful of any nut butter. Add banana, strawberries, blueberries — or even kiwi fruit or fresh pineapple.

Source: Goldie Caughlan, nutrition education manager at PCC Natural Markets in Seattle

effects and compromise cognitive development and school performance. "Healthy students are better able to develop and learn," reports the organization in its 2002 document "Commitment to Change."

Are America's school kids eating well? Probably not, contends Kathleen Mahan, owner of Nutrition by Design, a counseling service that specializes in children's nutrition. "Kids don't get enough protein," Mahan says. "That's what they need for building bodies, for blood glucose management, and for growing."

### What to pack

So what should you tuck into your child's lunch box? Peanut butter, the old lunch staple, has tumbled off the school-lunch list. While it's an excellent protein source (especially when made without hydrogenated fats), many schools have gone "peanut free" because of the rising number of children with peanut allergies. So Mahan recommends parents pack egg, tuna, or salmon salad, or turkey, along with low-fat string cheese or hummus.

Every lunch should include a fruit and a vegetable. Add a bag of baby carrots, an apple, sliced cucumbers or celery, and half a peach, Mahan suggests. "And keep the sweets small — no more than two Oreos." Better still is a homemade treat that includes butter or oil instead of hydrogenated fats.

Dietician Beverly Pressey, M.S., R.D., advises parents to offer children a variety of foods in their lunches. "Include choices they don't eat regularly, because it takes kids eight to ten times before they become familiar with a given food," says Pressey, the author of *Simple and Savvy Strategies for Creating Healthy Eaters.* "Pack whatever you would like them to eat. Eventually, they'll try it."

Pressey suggests adding non-sandwich selections, such as cold pasta with olive oil, soy nuts, cheese chunks, or — her idea of a perfect lunch — great bread with olive oil, a slice of cheese, and an apple.

A well-balanced meal — one that includes some protein, fats, and carbohydrates — helps kids stay full longer and improves their concentration. "If they're not hungry, it's easier for them to maintain their focus," Pressey says. "Once they start thinking about food, they lose it."

Keep sugary products at home — it ruins a child's appetite for more nutritious choices — and eliminate the juice boxes, Pressey says. "Juice is a concentrated sugar food. Your child will feel full after drinking it — and have no reason to eat anything more."

### Raising the bar

Caughlan notes that grocery shelves are already beginning to reflect the new government guidelines and the end of the "carbohydrate as enemy" trend. "You're seeing more whole-grain pasta, more whole grain in cereals," she says.

The National School Lunch Program, which provides low-cost or free lunches to children in public or nonprofit schools, has also raised the nutrition bar, with new and improved nutrient standards for school breakfast and lunch menus.

And parents are trying to prepare school lunches and family meals with greater dietary awareness, Caughlan says, even though buying fresh fruits and vegetables, cleaning them, chopping them, and trying to think of ways to get the family to eat them takes both effort and planning.

But it's important that parents keep plugging, planning, and chopping away. "If a parent stays involved and packs her child's lunch, it says, 'I thought about you, and I care about what you're eating,'" Mahan says.

## Q & A WITH ALICE WATERS

*Alice Waters, founder and owner of Chez Panisse in Berkeley, California, is the author of eight books, including* Chez Panisse Cooking, The Edible Schoolyard, *and* Fanny at Chez Panisse.

**Q: What's wrong with the way we approach food and eating in this country?**

It's clear that we as a nation don't know where our food comes from, and we don't know how to eat. The fast-food corporations have sold us a bill of goods. We don't know — as every other culture does — anything about the production of food, its relationship to agriculture, or its role in cultural traditions. We know of it as fueling up, and that it has something to do with our health. It is all very vague.

**Q: What does the way we eat tell us about ourselves?**

We've been taught a set of values by the foods that we eat. We've learned well about fast, cheap, and easy. And it's not just about food, but also about the way we think.

Your senses are the pathways into your mind and they tell you things about food. When you are touching, smelling, tasting, and looking, it opens up these pathways. But we have been closed down. Everything is packaged, wrapped, and sanitized. We are isolated in our cars and we aren't experiencing nature. It's very disorienting for children. Not eating together, for example, is a cultural crisis as well as a health and environmental crisis.

**Q: What should we teach our children about food?**

We need to bring children, at a very early age, into a relationship with food in an interactive way that helps them discover for themselves about where their food comes from. It's about reconnecting them to nature and to the culture of the table. We need to do this for health reasons, for environmental reasons, and to create the kind of place at the table where we can communicate with each other.

**Q: What are some ways to do that?**

Go to a farmers market and take your kids. Examine and touch the food together and let your kids help you plan a menu and cook. Children love to be out in nature. The engagement in growing and preparing food gives them a sense of empowerment and pride. You can create a garden with them in the backyard, plant some seeds in a box, or harvest food in someone else's garden. When they grow it and cook it, they want to eat it. It gives children a sense of responsibility and helps strengthen their relationship with nature.

Eating second-rate fruits and vegetables year-round dulls the palate. When my own daughter, Fanny, was young, I planted things I knew she'd like and that she could pick right out of the garden — even edible flowers. She'd be out there, even on her own, smelling and tasting.

**Q: While we know organic, locally grown foods are ideal, how can today's busy parents find time to shop for these foods and ingredients?**

They have to decide that they think this is important enough to do. The truth is it's easy to go to the market and find fruits and vegetables in season — then it takes nothing to cook. Don't forget about garlic — as they say, "Garlic is as good as ten mothers." Throw garlic in wintergreens and olive oil and vinegar; there isn't a kid who doesn't want to eat it.

**Q: What kinds of lunches did you typically pack for your daughter, Fanny, when she was in school?**

I always packed her salads and a container of vinaigrette. I'd make different salads every day: carrots with raisins; cherry tomatoes, big leaves of romaine to dip, oranges. I'd include garlic toast, pita bread, a hard-boiled egg. It always changed, or at least looked different. If she didn't eat something, I'd ask her why. But she always loved her lunch. I cared about what I prepared and I thought about it ahead of time. If we had chicken for dinner, I'd save part of it for a chicken salad. It's not hard and it's not rocket science; it just takes a little planning.

**Q: What additional advice can you offer parents about food and nutrition?**

I think that health and nutrition come from a really pleasurable relationship with food, one that's connected to human experience and to nature. The more you create that sort of prepared classroom — the classroom of the table or the garden — the more likely a child will come into it and find the things he needs to be healthy. Telling kids not to eat this and not to eat that — taking away something without bringing something else really beautiful in its place — is a recipe for disaster. When you put kids in charge of the meal, whether they're planning it or doing something fun and a little dangerous like cooking tortillas over the fire, it gives them a sense of responsibility. And the more they do that, the more they'll want to eat what they helped plan or prepare.

**RECIPE** **From *Fanny at Chez Panisse: A Child's Restaurant Adventures with 46 Recipes***

**Cherry Tomato Pasta**

2 baskets cherry tomatoes (about 5 cups)
1 cup extra virgin olive oil
1 tablespoon red wine vinegar
Fresh basil or parsley
Salt and pepper
3/4 to 1 pound dry linguine
Optional: 1 1/2 cups fresh breadcrumbs

While a big pot of water heats to boiling, prepare the tomatoes. Slice the tomatoes in half. Put them in a big bowl and add the olive oil and vinegar. Chop fresh basil or parsley and add to the tomatoes. Season with salt and pepper. Stir and let it sit for a while.

Cook the noodles and drain them, then add to the bowl of tomatoes. Mix well and serve on plates, spooning the tomatoes and juices over the noodles.

Add breadcrumbs at the end: Toast the fresh breadcrumbs on a cookie sheet in the oven until browned. Toss with a little olive oil and mix into the noodles and tomatoes.

CHAPTER 4

# Emotional Readiness Counts

## TEACHING KINDNESS AND EMPATHY

We live in a world that's downright daunting. Expressions like "lockdown" and "road rage" have become part of the American lexicon. Fear-driven parents are left to search far and wide for safe havens for their children; havens where troubles melt like lemon drops and predators don't lurk in cyberspace.

When most of today's parents were growing up, they biked solo around the neighborhood, walked alone and unarmed to the school bus stop, and stayed with unseasoned thirteen-year-old baby-sitters who came without background checks.

We get that the times, they are a-changin', but most of us met the twenty-first century unprepared for the increased dangers and threats that seem to lurk everywhere. We wonder: Where has all the kindness gone? And how do we get it back?

One way to start, educators say, is by teaching our children social values such as self-discipline, respect, and, perhaps most important of all, empathy.

Here's the thinking: If kids learn to understand how others think and feel, they will better understand how their choices affect them and their peers. Ideally, they'll grow up with a mindset that rejects hostility and violence.

"The idea is to decrease aggressive behaviors and increase social competence," says Claudia Glaze, director of client relations for Committee for Children, an international organization that develops curricula that focus on youth violence, bullying and personal safety, child abuse, and literacy.

Committee for Children created Second Step, a program that teaches social-emotional skills such as empathy, impulse control, and anger management to kids between ages four and fourteen. The programs are used throughout the United States and in Canada, northern Europe, and Japan.

Second Step is based on the premise that qualities such as empathy can be learned at school and at home. "When kids learn to take another person's perspective, they have an 'aha!' moment," notes Joan Cole Duffell, executive director of Committee for Children. "They suddenly realize they're not the only person in the room."

**Born to empathize?**

Researchers studying the biological origin of empathy have found that infants are born with the ability to imitate. We've all seen it: the newborn who copies his dad's facial expression; the baby who shakes the rattle just like her mother. That kind of imitation lays the foundation for empathy, scientists say.

"We believe that when infants imitate, they are becoming 'like the other person' in action, with simple body movements," says Andrew Meltzoff, Ph.D., codirector of I-LABS at the University

**TIPS TEACHING KINDNESS AND EMPATHY**

- Expand your child's emotional intelligence by asking often, "How do you feel?"
- Know what your child is watching and listening to; protect him from cruel, desensitizing images that can corrupt his empathic development.
- Point out the positive impact empathy can have on others.
- Tune up your empathic behaviors so your child sees you show concern for other people's needs.
- Act on your concern to comfort others, so your child can copy your actions.
- Provide opportunities for your child to experience different perspectives and views by visiting places such as nursing homes, homeless shelters, pediatric wards, and soup kitchens.

Source: *Building Moral Intelligence* by Michele Borba

of Washington. "Later, that can flower into empathy, which is the ability to become like the other person in emotion and perspective."

What does all this mean? The capacity for imitation is already wired into the DNA; our job is to help it grow into real emotional empathy and the ability to be compassionate. Meltzoff suggests parents begin nurturing empathy by playing imitative, reciprocal games with their babies. These can include using simple facial expressions such as opening their mouths, thrusting out their tongues — even just smiling. A few months later, parents can wave to their babies and play "peek-a-boo."

As babies get older, talk to them about their day — and really listen to what they say, advises David A. Levine, author of *Teaching Empathy: A Blueprint for Caring, Compassion, and Community.* Levine calls this "high-level" listening.

"Ask open-ended questions, such as 'Help me understand what happened,'" Levine says. "Put effort and energy into understanding what your child or someone else went through. Then reflect back his or her feelings with a comment like 'You must have been really disappointed.'"

Encourage kids to see other points of view. Say to your child, "How would you feel if that were you? What would you do?"

Read books to your children that deal with feelings. "Engage in a dialogue about the book," Duffell says. "Ask your child, 'How do you think this person is feeling now?'"

Find ways for your kids to show care and concern for others. "Maybe a neighbor is ill. Ask your children, 'How do we want to show him we care?'" suggests Glaze. "As they get older, help them find volunteer activities. Help them recognize kindness in all its forms."

And support school programs that help build social and emotional skills. "Not every child learns those skills at home. You can't assume every parent is mature; some are kids themselves," Duffell says.

Schools must attend to the whole child. "As citizens of the world's most powerful country, kids in the United States need to learn how to stand in other people's shoes," says Duffell. "After all, one day these kids may be sitting at a negotiating table."

## Q & A WITH ALFIE KOHN

*Alfie Kohn is the author of eleven books, including* Unconditional Parenting, Punished by Rewards, *and* The Brighter Side of Human Nature (*alfiekohn.org*).

**Q: How do we teach children social and emotional competence?**

We should distinguish between social and emotional "competence," on the one hand, which suggests a series of skills, and social or emotional dispositions, on the other hand, which imply a desire to do things such as express one's feelings, connect with other people, and so on. The latter is harder to teach and often overlooked. Lots of kids know how to be appropriately assertive, or how to help people in need, or how to read. The trouble is they often don't do these things that they're capable of doing.

Most programs that focus on social and emotional issues are about improving or fixing individual kids: trying to help them manage their anger, or empathize with others, or resolve conflicts effectively. What interests me even more, however, are the structural features of a classroom or school that end up encouraging or discouraging kids from learning how to do these things or wanting to do them.

**Q: Can social or emotional competence be taught in schools?**

Consider the current exaggerated focus on academic skills — or, worse, standardized test scores — to the exclusion of attending to other facets of children. School mission statements that mention the "whole child," or programs that teach educators how to promote children's emotional growth, won't have much effect if administrators or legislators are leaning on everyone to improve test scores. The single most important thing we can do right now to advance children's development, therefore, may be to join the growing grassroots resistance to the whole "accountability" fad that's turning our schools into glorified test-prep centers.

Another structural example derives from the importance of helping kids to experience their classrooms and schools as caring communities, places where they feel connected to — and safe with — their peers and adults, where they come to think in the plural ("It's about us, not just me") and feel a sense of belonging.

There are various ways to do this, including activities that have kids of different ages working together. But I'm also interested in what gets in the way. I sometimes ask teachers, rather perversely, how they would destroy a sense of community if for some reason they wanted to do so. Their answers include programs that segregate and stratify, such as tracking, ability grouping, and honors classes; and contests and other competitive practices that teach kids to view others as obstacles to their own success, including spelling bees, awards assemblies, and class rank.

**Q: Many parents say they just want their children to "be happy." Where do qualities such as respect, humility, and honesty fit into that?**

The psychoanalyst Erich Fromm once said, "Few parents have the courage and independence to care more for their children's happiness than for their success." So I give points to any parents who really support their children's choices that bring contentment, even if that's at the expense of good grades, public recognition, and making lots of money. Research has shown that when parents are more concerned about their kids' achievement than with their well-being, the kids' emotional health tends to suffer.

But happiness isn't enough. We also want to raise children who are concerned with whether other people are happy. I don't think we want kids to be so focused on their own well-being that they're indifferent to other people's suffering. Nor would I want happiness to be purchased at the price of a child's being unreflective, shallow, or unable to become outraged about outrageous things.

**Q: What can parents do to raise empathic, compassionate children?**

First, we need to care about them. All instruction and intervention has to be nested in a relationship that feels warm, safe, and unconditionally loving to the child. The same words keep coming up in guidelines for raising a moral child that are offered by different experts: secure attachment, nurturance, respect, responsiveness, and empathy. When these basic human needs are met, a child is freed from having to be preoccupied with them and can be open to helping others. But if these needs are not met, they may continue to reverberate in the child's ears, with the result that he or she is deaf to other people's cries of distress.

That care must be unconditional. We need to love kids for who they are, not for what they do. They should know they still mean the world to us even when they mess up or fall short. Our love should never be something children feel they have to earn. That basic principle helps to explain why punishments (like "time out," which is experienced as a form of love withdrawal) and rewards (including verbal rewards — "Good job!") prove to be so counterproductive. These are techniques of conditional parenting, not unconditional.

Second, show them how a moral person lives. Even before they're steady on their feet, children are soaking up our values. They're learning from us how to be a human being. Parents who want to teach the importance of honesty make it a practice never to lie to their children, even when it would be easier just to claim that there are no cookies left rather than to explain why the child can't have another one.

Third, let them practice. Give kids plenty of opportunities to help so they come to define themselves as helpful people.

Finally, talk with them about moral issues. It's not enough for us to have good values; these values must be communicated directly and in a way that's fitted to the child's ability to understand. The use of reason promotes independent thought and makes it clear that while we want to influence our children, we also want them to think for themselves. And that requires us to engage in real conversations. The most impressive moral growth takes place in children whose parents don't just talk *at* them, but engage in dialogues with them.

## UNDERSTANDING YOUR CHILD'S TEMPERAMENT

Maybe your child is turning out to be just what you'd envisioned: a bona fide mini-you whose personality blends in graceful harmony with yours.

Then again, maybe not. Perhaps your child is outgoing, gregarious, and intense — but friends describe you as "reserved." Or maybe your four-year-old is afraid to tackle the playground ladder. You, on the other hand, have led climbing expeditions in the Himalayas.

New parents find out quickly that babies come prewired — and that there's not much they can do to change those fundamental, built-in qualities that make up what we call a child's "temperament."

"When that little bundle arrives home, you're already beginning to see inclinations that child has," says Sandra Looper, a former elementary school teacher and principal. "All children come with a predisposition toward people and toward their environment. And that predisposition may or may not correlate with that of their parents."

What happens when a child's temperament doesn't match a parent's expectations? Experts call that a "poorness of fit" and say it can affect a child's development — particularly if parents don't accept that child for who he or she is.

Child development specialists describe a variety of temperament traits commonly found in children. Researchers often cite the work of child psychiatrists and authors Alexander Thomas and Stella Chess, who identified nine temperament characteristics that can be present from birth:

1. **Activity level:** Is your child relaxed, or constantly on the go?
2. **Rhythmicity:** How does your child sleep? Eat? Are there noticeable patterns?
3. **Approach/withdrawal:** Is your child eager for new experiences, or shy and hesitant?
4. **Adaptability:** Is he able to adjust to changes and transitions?
5. **Sensory threshold:** Is he bothered by loud noises? Bright lights? Certain food textures?
6. **Intensity:** Does he react strongly to situations?
7. **Quality of mood:** Is he negative and pessimistic, or positive and hopeful?
8. **Distractibility:** Can your child stick with activities?
9. **Persistence:** How quickly does he give up?

### Parents can help shape temperament

Parents have their own ideas about which personality traits count, and often focus on their child's irritability and energy level, and whether their children can adapt to new situations. Above all, they worry when their kids appear to be shy.

"In this country, we have a cultural bias toward a particular personality we call 'Type A' — we admire it," says Sherry Catron Wong, director of research and development at Committee for

**TIPS** **UNDERSTANDING YOUR CHILD'S TEMPERAMENT**

- Help your child try things that may not come naturally.
- Talk to your child about her temperament and help her understand it.
- Help your child figure out ways to adjust to different situations.
- Focus on the positive aspects of your child's personality and temperament.
- Don't pin labels on your child.

Children. "People think, 'If my child's too shy, she won't do well.'"

While a child's disposition is largely inborn, parents still have the ability to shape and influence it by paying attention to behavior, personality, and communication cues. It's the interactions between temperament and environment that count, experts say.

At the same time, children must learn to function outside the home. That means a shy child needs to try new things; a take-charge child needs to let others have a turn; a highly distractible child needs to be able to sit through a class. Teaching kids to adapt to the world while respecting their innate abilities is like "walking a parenting tightrope," Looper says. "Our parenting styles — how we react to behaviors and temperament — can have a tremendous influence on developing our children's personalities."

It helps to talk to children about their own temperaments. Ask them to think through ways they can adjust to different situations. It also helps to plan ahead. Prepare your shy child to know what to expect by explaining what's about to happen: "Mommy is going to leave you at preschool and then come back."

And focus on the positive. What looks like a problem today might be an advantage tomorrow. Is your son easily distracted? As a student, that's a negative — but as a future video game designer, that's a plus. Or maybe your daughter's persistence drives you nuts. That same determination might drive her to solve complex math equations. Above all, avoid labeling. Don't say, "This is my shy one, this is my athlete."

"Parents tend to attach labels to their children — and blame certain traits for any issues they have," says Wong. "But this is only one part of who the child is."

## CREATING CALM THROUGH REFLECTIVE PARENTING*

The battle lines are drawn, and you are facing off against a formidable foe: your child. Whatever you're arguing about, you've been down this road before. Why does your child behave this way? Frustration mounts as you struggle to keep your temper in check.

Welcome to yet another white-knuckle moment in parenting. We've all been there, and most of us know that how we handle these moments — these conflicts — is important. But what can a harried parent do in the heat of the moment? And if we blow it in this moment, can we turn back the clock later when we're calm?

The answer for some parents may lie in an approach to child-rearing called "reflective parenting." Simply put, reflective parenting is interacting with your child while keeping a close eye on his — and your — state of mind and emotion. It's empathy, patience, and intuition all rolled into one.

Increasing your reflective thinking can bring about a greater understanding of your child and can give you skills to diffuse those "white-knuckle" moments, says Arietta Slade, Ph.D., a clinical psychologist and researcher at Yale Child Study Center. And the good news is, she says, it's already within each of us to some degree, and there are small and simple things we can do to bring it out.

"Every parent has the capacity to think reflectively," says Slade. "Whether they do or don't is based on a lot of different factors, including how stressed they are, how overloaded they are in life." Reflectiveness is something that comes and goes, she says. "If you're completely overwhelmed with feelings, you are less likely to be reflective."

Reflective thinking begins by realizing that that little alien you've created has a deep, rich inner life all his own. Think of your child as an interesting person that you would like to get to know. John Grienenberger, Ph.D., founder of the Reflective Parenting Program in Los Angeles, says keeping this in mind is key to understanding where your child is coming from in those white-knuckle moments.

* By Kristen Russell Dobson, managing editor of *ParentMap* magazine

"One of the reasons parenting is so difficult," Grienenberger says, "is that it involves two contradictory capacities: One is to be able to understand the connection between ourselves and our children, and the other is to remember that our child is a separate being." Reflective functioning, he explains, is about realizing there are two individuals — the parent and the child — who are inextricably intertwined, but are not the same.

Spend a little time thinking about that separate little being. What is really behind that frustrating behavior? Is your child clinging to your leg because he wants his own way? Or is it something deeper than that — a fear of strangers, perhaps, or a wish to spend more time with you? It's not hard for harried, hurried parents to slip into a kind of adversarial thinking about their child's motivations, Slade says. Often, the simple act of slowing down brings insights. Slade calls this "holding your child in mind."

### How you affect your child

Next, take a close look at your own behavior. "Parents have a hard time dealing with the fact that if they are angry or stressed, that's going to have an impact on their child," says Slade. "They want to think that if they put them in the right program and take them to gym and music, what's going on inside of themselves isn't going to affect their children."

She suggests parents reflect on their own history and goals for their child. For most of us, stress is inevitable; how you cope with your own stress has a big effect on your children, says Slade.

This kind of thinking takes time and patience — something you don't have in the heat of battle. But even if you blow it during a blow-up, you'll get a second chance, says Grienenberger. "Blow-ups can be readdressed later. Reflective thinking is also about that 'aha' moment that happens hours after an argument, when you sit down and talk about what happened." This talk isn't necessarily about solving problems, says Grienenberger, but about calmly describing and discussing what happened with your child, giving him more of a sense of self-control.

So, the next time you're locked in battle, pause, take a deep breath, and notice that you're engaged in something right now, says Grienenberger. Acknowledge those high emotions to your child. "Sometimes parents can just comment on what they're seeing:

**TIPS REFLECTIVE PARENTING**

- Remember that your child is a separate being.
- Slow down and think about what's really behind your child's behavior.
- Pay attention to your own feelings.
- Think about ways to cope with your stress and anger.
- Talk with your child about emotions — yours and your child's.
- Give your child fifteen minutes a day of your undivided attention.
- Don't teach or preach during those fifteen minutes.

'There are some big feelings here now, and I think this is about more than just can you have another cookie.'" And remember, as parents, we often don't even notice the things that cause our children stress. But their stress is valid — even if we don't understand it.

You can help create a culture of calm and reflection in your house by giving your child just fifteen minutes a day of your undivided attention, Slade and Grienenberger say. Tell your child you're going to spend some time together doing something they choose — then turn off your cell phone and play. Pay attention to how your child engages with you and don't teach or correct. "When families do this, it's stunning sometimes the impact that those few minutes have on children being more calm and regulated," says Grienenberger.

"Some parents hate it, because it's not goal-oriented," says Slade. "But turn off your cell phone, get someone to watch the sibling. It's hard to do — but the payoff is great!"

## Q & A WITH YAFFA MARITZ

*Yaffa Maritz is a psychologist and the clinical director of the Listening Mothers and Reflective Parenting programs.*

**Q: What does it mean to be a "reflective parent"?**

A reflective parent is a parent who is able to think about and explore both the meaning behind their child's behavior, as well as what triggers their own reactions to their children. Reflective parents have developed skills that heighten their awareness of both their child's emotions and feelings, and their own. They tend to be curious about the "emotional story" behind the behavior, and are able to help the kids name feelings and brainstorm solutions, if needed. Reflecting about feelings leads to the ability to regulate and manage feelings, rather than feeling hijacked by them and out of control.

**Q: How does this increase our understanding of our children?**
Reflective parents understand that their child's behavior is triggered by his or her unique experience. Therefore, the parent understands that the child is a separate individual with a mind, wishes, desires, motivations, and emotions of his own. Being able to accept the child as he is helps parents respond to their child with sensitivity without feeling threatened by that child's intense emotions or defiant behavior.

**Q: Why is this important?**
A child's healthy emotional development and secure attachment is the foundation for his lifelong well-being. Children thrive in an environment where they feel understood, connected, and loved. Reflective parents teach their children, through modeling and direct interaction, that their behavior has meaning worth exploring, that emotions can be regulated, that trust and mutual respect are built through consistency in daily interaction, and that we learn from successes as well as from failures.

**Q: What can parents do to be more aware and "mindful" of our feelings and those of our children?**
Learning to become mindful is a lifelong skill — one that's worth developing! One must become committed to the journey of becoming mindful, self-aware, and centered — and be able to regulate one's own emotions. It is a journey rather than a destination, and it takes different routes depending on what works for the individual. As the parents venture on this journey, the kids will follow. And just as parents can't expect themselves to be consistently "mindful," they will have empathy for their kids' struggle with "doing it right" all the time!

**Q: Roots of Empathy, a classroom program that began in Canada, helps reduce aggression in schoolchildren by increasing empathy. How does the program work?**

The heart of the Roots of Empathy program (*rootsofempathy.org*) is an infant and parent who visit a classroom once every three weeks throughout the school year. A trained Roots of Empathy instructor visits the classroom the week before the baby's visit for a pre-lesson and the week after the baby's visit for a post-lesson.

The instructor guides the students to observe the relationship between the infant and parent, to talk about their own feelings, and to deepen their understanding of temperament and human development. Concepts and experiences are reinforced through artwork, writing, and carefully selected children's books. Students become very attached to "their" baby. Through the power of the baby, students have a unique opportunity to learn about perspective, differences, milestones, and feelings.

**Q: Can we really teach our children empathy and compassion?**

Children are born with a sense of empathy and compassion. Dr. Andy Meltzoff, codirector of the University of Washington I-LABS, has shown it with his work with kids as young as eighteen months old. When these young children see someone hurting himself with a sharp object, their faces crumble with pain.

We all know that babies start crying when they see another baby cry. But if kids don't grow up in an environment where their feelings are attended to, if their emotions are ignored or dismissed, they learn to shut off the part of them that's in touch with their own emotions — as well as their ability to feel compassion for others.

## HELPING THE RISK-AVERSE CHILD

Some kids seem fearless. They bounce from one activity to another, eager to be the first on the monkey bars, the first up at bat, and the first to offer the solution to the algebra problem — whether it's the right one or not.

If that sounds like your child, stop reading right here and hand this page to your friend — the one with the son or daughter the experts like to call "risk averse." This is the kid who needs to be pushed to try new things; who will answer a question in class with

"I don't know" rather than risking a wrong reply; who's reluctant to pick up the bat because she might strike out.

Failure, for these children, is not an option.

Why do some kids seem to approach transitions and challenges with ease, while others find the same situations scary and intimidating?

Lots of factors — temperament, upbringing, environment — come into play. "Some children are more naturally eager to try new things, while others may be more reluctant," says Chris Ladish, Ph.D., head of Pediatric Psychology and Psychiatry Service at Mary Bridge Children's Hospital in Tacoma, Washington. While most kids recognize there's an element of the unknown in new tasks, they don't necessarily steer clear of them. But for certain children, just the thought of trying something new brings on anxiety.

### Setting the stage

Often, early experiences help set the stage for the way kids view challenges later on. For example, if they've received parental support only when they succeed, chances are they aren't set up to handle failure, according to Cora Collette Breuner, M.D., M.P.H., an attending physician in adolescent medicine at Seattle Children's Hospital. And

### TIPS SUPPORTING RISK-AVERSE KIDS

- Emphasize effort as much as outcome. Praise the fact that your child tries.
- Take breaks. None of us is at our best when pushed beyond our limits.
- End on positive notes. Divide complex tasks into smaller, more doable segments and celebrate the completion of each.
- Create a healthy balance between challenging projects and tasks and easy ones. Review the day with your child.
- Spend time talking about success. Catch the child doing things "right." The more a child hears and receives praise for positive efforts, the more that child will come to internalize that message.
- Embrace failure and help your child to not be afraid of it. We all had to fall many times before we learned to walk.

depending upon the way success is defined at home and at school, "success" to some might mean "failure" to others. Is success about playing the game or about winning? About attempting the puzzle or about matching all the pieces? About tackling the math problem or getting 100 percent? "Is it the effort or the outcome? You can have a failed outcome, but success in terms of putting forth your best efforts," Ladish says.

Some risk-averse children suffer from self-esteem issues and resist trying new things if they're out of their comfort zone. For those kids, it helps when teachers assure them there's more than one "right" way to do things.

It also helps to encourage risk-averse kids to value the process, not just the result. That might mean giving them smaller, simpler challenges until they build up their self-confidence. "The message both from home and from teachers should be that it's OK not to be able to do something right away," says Wilder Dominick, the head of Open Window School in the Seattle area. Focus on 'I'm so proud you tried that.'"

And don't overdo it on the praise. "Praise should not be contingent upon success, but on giving it your best shot," says Breuner. "Your kid is great whether she runs around with a bucket on her head or is Clara in *The Nutcracker.*"

## HOW MUCH IS TOO MUCH?

My Barbie doll had a blond ponytail, blue eyes, and perfect proportions. I coveted this doll. She's still here, tucked away in a blue faux-leather Barbie box, along with her dazzling duds: a shimmering black gown, a creamy hostess outfit, and a black-and-white, zebra-striped bathing suit.

I realize this recollection places me in a long-ago and faraway childhood, when every Rolling Stones or Bob Dylan album I bought was a big deal (you couldn't download hundreds of them onto your iPod) and when kids made do with single dolls, dresses, and toys, instead of infinite sets of them.

These days, who buys just one Barbie? Who buys just one anything? Even families struggling with tighter budgets and challenging new economic realities work hard to keep their kids knee deep in stuff. But experts say those efforts are often misguided.

Parent educator Elizabeth Crary, the author of more than 60 books and articles for parents and children, advises parents and caretakers to draw the line at overindulgence. "Overindulged kids lose self-esteem," Crary says. "They'll feel they're only valuable if they have the newest jacket or the latest PlayStation."

They miss the chance to build important skills, she says: how to budget, how to decide whether to buy the blue shirt or the red shirt.

Think your kids appreciate the collection of games, books, and toys that fill your living room or playroom? Don't count on it. It turns out, the more they have, the more they want. "Children raised in

## TIPS PREVENTING OVERINDULGENCE

- Assign chores.
- Establish a clothing allowance. Once it's spent, it's spent.
- Let your child suffer the consequences of her actions. If she is mean to a friend, let her resolve the problem.
- Figure out how many shirts, pants, and pairs of shoes your child needs. Then make rules about what she can own.
- Have her do something for the community, and make sure it's a true interaction. Pick a project like cleaning up a stream; let your child plan it and work it out.
- Be a good role model. Ask yourself: What kind of person do you want your child to grow up to be?
- Connect your money to the responsibility that comes with it and the effort it took to earn.
- Use an allowance to teach money management and to help your child understand that there are limits to spending.
- Teach your child the difference between what she wants and what she needs.
- Expect your child to work outside the family to understand the connection between work and money.
- Make sure your child establishes financial independence as a young adult; cut the financial "umbilical cord."
- Avoid the "trust-fund syndrome" — when kids get money they had no involvement in earning.

Sources: Parent educators Elizabeth Crary and Barbara Swenson

the midst of too much stuff don't do well," says Barbara Swenson, a Seattle-area parent educator. "They get distracted, demanding, whiny, and entitled. And they think they are entitled to even more."

Sometimes the catering, pampering, and pleasing are more about the parent than the child. When's the last time you saw a two-year-old angle for an $800 stroller, or a Burberry raincoat, or a pair of Italian party shoes? "Maybe the parents want to show off to their friends. Maybe they didn't get everything when they were kids," says Crary.

One mother told Swenson that her daughter's closet was crammed with clothing, some with tags still attached. "The mother seemed proud of this," Swenson says.

That kind of überconsumerism puts pressure on less-affluent communities and on parents who struggle with tight budgets. "The kids from poorer areas have to have the trendy stuff, too," says Swenson. "Parents with low budgets try to keep up. When they can't provide for their kids at that level, they feel inadequate."

#### Need versus want

An overemphasis on materialism increases kids' expectations. Kids learn they can have what they want — and there are parents who don't see why they shouldn't give it to them.

Do they need a new Nintendo DS when the one they have still works, or do they simply want it? Do they know the difference? "A long time ago, parents would say, 'You can earn the money for this, and we'll pay half.' Now kids don't learn to work for what they want," says Crary. "These parents are setting their children up for unreasonable expectations for the future."

They're also promoting questionable values that can surface at school. "I see kids trying to buy friends with the latest gadget, with the family pool, with the new Mercedes they got for their birthday," Swenson says.

Some families equate money with power, and feel their wealth should buy their children good grades — minus the effort. These kids may or may not achieve top grades. What they will achieve, however, is an unmistakable feeling of entitlement.

"Just because you can give your children more things, more trips, more lessons doesn't mean it's good for them," she says. When your child has everything and still begs for more, it's time to ditch the checkbook. "They don't have to have it all," says Swenson. "They should want for something."

CHAPTER 5

# Solving School Dilemmas

■ ■ ■ ■ ■

## COPING WITH FAILURE

Second-grader Lolly, an early reader, relished books and delighted in getting picked to read to the other students. She loved being in the "fast-track" reading group — until one day, she wasn't. Her comprehension skills, it turned out, needed some work. Lolly was devastated.

It's no fun to lose. Even if your child typically wins, chances are at some point, he'll feel the pain of being overlooked for the baseball team; of misspelling a word during the spelling bee; of bungling the geometry exam that was supposed to be a slam-dunk.

Or maybe not. Maybe your kid is the one who always gets the A, wins the election, and wows the coach. But those kids are rather rare; let's call them "imaginary." Most children run up against assorted speed bumps and setbacks along the long and winding road to becoming grownups.

That's why families need to be equipped with tools that will help their children cope with failure, even if failure only happens once in a while.

"When things go wrong, some parents want a quick fix — and who wouldn't?" says Susan Small, director of student services at Educational Tutoring and Consulting, a Seattle-area tutoring company. "They'd like to put a simple Band-Aid on the problem."

But a thoughtful approach works better than the fast fix, she says. For starters, parents should identify the problem their child is facing. Is there a pattern, or is it an isolated event?

"The response will be different if the student is dealing with ongoing concerns, such as attention deficit disorder or learning disabilities," Small says. Parents who suspect their child has a learning disability should seek help from their child's pediatrician, teacher, and the school psychologist.

If it's a single incident, try to find out what caused it. Were expectations too high? Were there family issues? Social stressors?

Take, for example, that first report card — the one with real letter grades instead of those carefully couched comments kids get in elementary school. For the first time, kids are getting real feedback on their performance. While grades can motivate some students, they can upset others.

**Ask the right questions**

It's up to parents to ask their children the right questions. If your child got a bad grade, find out why. Ask your child, "Is your homework getting turned in? Is there enough test-prep going on? Did you understand the assignment?" After that, ask, "How can I help you?"

Stay positive. The standard clichés such as "You'll do better next time" or "You'll just study harder" don't give kids useful information; they just leave the kid feeling mystified, according to Karen Dickinson, a former associate superintendent for the Tacoma School District in Washington. What works better? Dickinson suggests giving the less-than-stellar score an upbeat spin: "You got a 60, which means you know 60 percent of the work. That's more than you don't know!"

**TIPS** **HELPING YOUR CHILD COPE WITH FAILURE**

- Identify the problem. Is there a pattern, or is it an isolated event?
- Try to find out what caused the problem. Were expectations too high? Were there family issues? Social stressors?
- Ask your child how you can help.
- Try to come up with solutions.
- Email the teacher for more information.
- Don't try to "rescue" your child.
- Praise your child for the good things she does.

Next, come up with solutions — as many of them as you can. This might mean making sure homework comes home and goes back to class when it's completed. It might mean buying a second set of textbooks, because your child keeps leaving hers at her desk, or simply having your child moved to a different location in the classroom.

Students often encounter their first hurdles in middle school when they find their old study habits don't measure up to increased expectations. Just memorizing facts won't cut it anymore; now the kids need to absorb the information and integrate it into their papers and discussions. How to help? Teach your kids to study and make sure they have a designated study spot at home.

Email the teacher if you want to get (or give) more information about your kids. But don't try to rescue them. Overzealous parents with a penchant for stepping in to "smooth things over" model lessons of a different sort. "Their children learn how to wiggle their way out of things," Small says. "Will it help them succeed? Probably. Get into college? Probably. Feed their soul and help their intellect? Probably not."

Older kids — those in middle school and high school — should conduct their own negotiations with teachers. This means discussions about whether the student will retake a test, do extra credit, or come in for help should start with the child, not the parent.

Remember to praise your children for the good things they do, Small says. "Let them know you love them, despite the glitches and the setbacks." Some of what you tell them will just roll off their back. "Say it anyway," she says. "They need to hear it; it's essential to their not giving up."

## Q & A WITH WENDY MOGEL, PH.D.

*Dr. Wendy Mogel is a clinical psychologist and the author of* The Blessing of a Skinned Knee.

**Q: How do parents view their kids' failures?**

Parents see their children's bumps in the road as their own failures. This is the dark side of parental devotion. Parents look at the economy, the schools, college competition, and the planet, and it makes them feel anxious. They narrow their focus to their child, and that's how they measure their worth and effectiveness as a parent. Their children's grades are their grades.

**Q: What's wrong with this perspective?**

It's an unreliable and inaccurate way of predicting their child's future. Parents think grades give them a snapshot of their child, and it is not true. Some parents start with their baby's Apgar scores, show off in Mommy & Me class, and continue this right through the SATs. It takes a kind of narcissism and vanity to want your kids to be so spectacular.

**Q: How does this affect children?**

When parents overvalue school achievement, the children feel like personal failures. They feel they are valued for their performance, instead of being valued for being a good person.

Today, many kids — who don't have to milk the cow or even do chores — feel that the only currency they can contribute to the family are their grades. They become so anxious that it interferes with their performance and ability to concentrate. Some kids feel their grades are what keep their parents' marriages together. They sense how focused their parents are on their success and they think good grades will raise their parents' spirits.

**Q: What's wrong with overindulging and overprotecting our kids?**

We treat children like handicapped royalty. Some kids have housekeepers to pick up their clothes and tutors to make sure they're keeping up in class. If you have your own private adult waiting for you after school with milk and cookies, you don't need to develop the courage to say to the teacher, "I'm sorry, I didn't understand that — could you explain?"

Kids who play a small part in the play now get a bouquet of roses. If they come home with artwork, parents scan it and send it to their entire email list. They grow up thinking everything they do is precious. The college deans call the incoming students "tea cups," because they are fragile from being so managed and cared for, or "crispies," because they are burned out from too much pressure, overscheduling, and overwork.

**Q: Is there an upside to failure?**

Without failure, there's no opportunity for kids to learn effective coping strategies and techniques. Good judgment comes from experience, and experience comes from bad judgment — from making mistakes. That's where you learn what works and doesn't work. With the overprotective parent who's always fixing things, you don't learn how to handle challenges. In real life, no one is fawning over you and telling you how wonderful you are.

I want the kids to have a crabby, uninspired, unenlightened fourth-grade teacher, because chances are, they'll one day have a difficult, uninspired boss.

**Q: How can parents help their children learn to cope?**

Parents should allow their kids to face the consequences of their choices. These days, when a child comes home with a B-minus, the parents call the teacher. But instead of asking, "Why did you give my child this grade?" they should be asking, "What can we do to support her so she will be able to tackle this material?"

Parents talk in code. In many schools you are not allowed to request a teacher, so parents will say, "Drew's learning style is such and such; I think he would be a good match for this teacher." Parents of middle-school girls will call another parent and ask why their child wasn't invited to the birthday party. But it's like life — we don't get invited to everything.

**Q: What's the solution?**

I'd like to see parents band together. They should support each other in not overprotecting and overindulging their children, and not expecting them to be good in everything. Let's remember that these are the leaders of the next generation.

## 'I'M BORED!'

When Danielle Kassow, Ph.D., was growing up, every now and then she'd grumble, "I'm bored!"

Few things irritated her mother more. "My mother would tell me, 'Go play; go find something to do!'" says Kassow, who has worked as a research associate at Talaris Institute and is now at Thrive by Five Washington, a public-private education partnership created to support early learning.

Not much has changed since Kassow was a child. Parents still loathe hearing the "B" word, and kids still pull it out of their complaint repertoire. Even in an iPod, Xbox, and DVD world, "bored" persists in the tot-through-teen lexicon.

What's more, the word means different things to different kids at different times. "Sometimes children say they're bored because they need direction or activity ideas from their parents," Kassow says. "And sometimes, it's a child's way of telling a parent, 'I want you to pay attention to me.'"

If a very young child says she's bored, she often means, "I don't like what I'm doing right now," early learning experts say. Then it's the parent's job to come up with ideas.

Create a list of conversation starters. Ask your preschooler, "What's your favorite book?" or "If you could buy anything at the grocery store, what would it be?" Give her little projects, such as counting how many apples are in the fridge or how many chairs are in the house.

If your child claims she's bored at school, translate that. "What does it really mean?" asks Bryan Taylor, president of Partnership for Learning, a national nonprofit that helps schools and communities work to boost learning. "Often, it's a signal that your child needs to be redirected."

Maybe she's trying to tell you her classwork isn't challenging. "What she might mean is, 'This doesn't engage me. There's no incentive to do this when I already know I can,'" Taylor says. On the other hand, she might need more guidance, says Taylor, as in "I kind of understand this, but I don't know where to start. There's no path for me to follow."

Let's say your child is doing a report on bees. The topic's interesting, and your child is enthusiastic about the project. But where — and how — does she begin?

That's where you come in. "Kids need coaches," says Taylor. "We should take that role whether we're the parent, the teacher, or the tutor." Help your child through the report process, step by step, he suggests. "Create a pathway for her so she can understand how to put the project in order."

Maybe your student's learning style doesn't jibe with the instructor's teaching style. The best way to find that out is by asking questions, Kassow says. "Ask your child, 'What's boring? What did you do for this lesson? Were you finished before the other kids?'"

**Helping kids wait**

On the other hand, the "bored" buzzword can mean something else entirely, says Elizabeth MacKenzie, Ph.D., a Seattle child and adolescent psychologist. "Sometimes it has to do with being independent and organizing activities," she says. "Kids these days haven't had practice entertaining themselves."

That's often because they've had too much screen time, she says. "Watching TV and playing video games are highly entertaining but passive activities." You don't need attention skills to use screens, and they won't help your children learn to sidestep boredom.

MacKenzie likes to help young children learn strategies to stay busy. "I ask them, 'What can you do to help yourself wait?'" She suggests activities kids can do by themselves, such as coloring and playing with Legos. She tells parents to set a timer for different amounts of time to get children used to playing alone.

The timer technique also works with homework, she says. "When kids doing homework need their parents too much, there are often conflicts," says MacKenzie. "A parent might say, 'You're not doing that right.'"

### TIPS HELPING YOUR 'BORED' CHILD

- Ask your child what she means when she says she's bored. Is the work too challenging — or is it too easy?
- Talk to your child's teacher. Are there other projects the teacher can give her?
- Determine if your child understands the assignments.
- Try to find out if your child is not paying attention or focusing and, if so, help her work on those skills.
- Consider the possibility that your child is making a bid for more attention from you.
- Turn off the electronics and get kids involved in old-fashioned play.

Sources: Elizabeth MacKenzie, Ph.D., and Danielle Kassow, Ph.D.

Set the timer for a bit longer than your children can normally work by themselves and help them plan their study agenda, she says. When the timer goes off, check on them, gradually increasing the time they spend alone.

Some kids who complain they're bored in school tend to focus on the negative, MacKenzie says. "They have a bad school attitude. When they constantly say school's boring or 'stupid,' it can be part of a pattern of negative thinking."

How can you help your kids change that? Ask them to tell you three good things about their day. Then ask them what they're looking forward to the next day. "Help them see that there's something positive that happens every day," says MacKenzie. "Sometimes they just don't see the good things."

## IS YOUR CHILD IN THE WRONG CLASS?

Those first-week back-to-school jitters were normal, you reasoned. And that first month? OK, it was difficult, but everyone knows some kids take extra time adjusting to the new school year. But now it's well into fall, your child starts the day in tears and comes home the same way, and you're beginning to suspect something more worrisome is going on.

Could it be that your child is in the wrong class?

Mismatches happen, particularly when parents' expectations are high, says Seattle educational counselor Carol Robins. "We expect one teacher and more than 20 kids to be in a relationship, learn from each other, respect each other's values and behaviors — all while communicating effectively and compassionately. What a challenge!"

It's a challenge schools take seriously, because the stakes are high. "It's hugely important that we make the right teacher and classroom connections," says Linda Robinson, a former principal with Seattle Public Schools. "The kids should be happy, and school should be a happy place."

That's why Robinson was always "obsessive," she says, about finding good fits for her school's kindergarten through fifth-grade students. To place students in the right classes, Robinson used a protocol that considers gender, learning style, ethnicity, academic achievement, special needs, and friendships.

### TIPS HANDLING A POSSIBLE CLASSROOM MISMATCH

- Be sensitive to your child's needs and concerns. Watch for behavioral changes, such as crying at the door, stomachaches, or sleeplessness.
- Try to solve problems with your child by talking to her about what's going on at school.
- Contact the teacher and tell her what your child is reporting.
- If things don't improve, meet with the teacher and principal, and express your concerns.
- Consider calling in a professional to observe the class.
- Work as a team to confront and resolve the issues.

Administrators and teachers must figure out which kids should be separated and which kids should stay together; which combinations of academics and personalities work best; and whether there's an even balance of boys and girls in each class, Robinson says.

It takes an extraordinary amount of effort to make all of those elements mesh. It also takes a bit of guesswork. Robinson color-coded every class list, wrote endless charts, and conferred with teachers. But not all of the process can be quantified. "In the end, I'd sit at home by myself and get a sense of the gestalt of this group of kids." What didn't Robinson do? She didn't accommodate parents who made special teacher or classroom requests. Even if problems arose mid-year, most students stayed in their original classes. "If there were issues, I'd work with the teacher," she says.

Birgit McShane would be the first to tell you every principal views student placement differently. "For me, there isn't a set rule," says McShane, a former elementary school principal. While McShane always tried to keep parents happy, she was well aware they could be swayed and influenced by the ever-present rumor mill. "Some parents march in and say, 'I just can't have this teacher,' and it's based on something they've heard," she says. "Parents get together and decide certain teachers are better."

And parents often misjudge their kids. They might, for example, demand their child learn division in math class, when the student has not yet mastered multiplication. Often, McShane says, they think their child's abilities are higher than they actually are.

Most educators aim for an effective student-classroom blend, while accommodating families when possible. That could mean placing a child who's been through foster homes with a "warm and fuzzy" teacher, or teaming a student up with an old-school, no-nonsense instructor because that's what the parent requests.

**Getting connected**

When should you get involved? If your child resists going to school, has trouble sleeping, gets tummy aches, or is acting out in an unusual way, it's time to step in. These are all signs that something's amiss and that parents should begin a dialogue with the child's teacher, the principal, or other parents.

If needed, call in professionals to observe the class and offer ideas for solutions. "Parents, kids, and professionals are all in this together, and it helps to work with people the child encounters each day," Robins says.

Parents need to know that everyone at school is on the child's side, says Mercer Island, Washington, school psychologist Beth Remy. "We confer with parents and school staff until we unravel the problem," says Remy. "We ask: 'Is there structure at home but not at school? Is there a mismatch between the child's developmental readiness and what we are asking the child to do?'"

The child may need to be evaluated for special emotional or academic needs, says McShane. "Some kids are perfectionists; they shut down and won't work. Others are very sensitive."

Ideally, the school and the parents find a way to make the teacher-student combo work. Sometimes that means the teacher fine-tunes the way he or she is interacting with a particular child, depending on that student's academic or emotional needs.

But let's say the teacher seems inflexible. What if things still aren't jelling? Then it's time to consider other options. But think long and hard before demanding a classroom switch. "What are you telling your child? If things don't work out, I'll rescue you?" Remy asks. Reserve the class changes for "terrible fits," she says. "If it's really a mismatch, that might be the solution."

## HELPING YOUR PROCRASTINATOR

How many of us never, ever put off until tomorrow what we can do today? Most of our closets aren't completely organized; our correspondence isn't entirely up to date. Yet, when our children dillydally over schoolwork, our tolerance level is slim to none.

We all practice the art of procrastination. But most of us have learned that, ultimately, we need to get the job done. And we want to make sure our children figure that out, too.

Some parents size up their little procrastinators early on, when their kids take their sweet time making their beds, washing the dishes, or moseying through other chores, notes Kirsten O'Malley, owner of The Learning Curve, a tutoring company in Issaquah, Washington. As these children grow older, they're often the ones parents can't pry from the Xbox, she says.

By the time they get to middle school, the young slowpokes find that old habits carry new consequences. "Assignments become longer and more complex, and teachers are less likely to accept late work," says O'Malley.

Frustrated parents resort to dramatic solutions such as nixing privileges or commanding them to "Just do the work!" O'Malley says. "They want to help their child succeed. From their perspective, their kids are shooting themselves in the foot. But the truth is, many of these kids have already tuned their parents out."

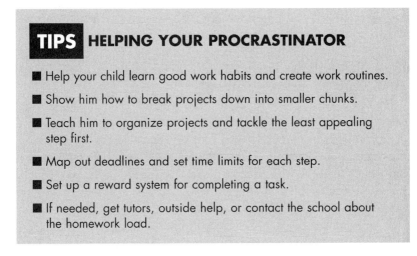

### TIPS HELPING YOUR PROCRASTINATOR

- Help your child learn good work habits and create work routines.
- Show him how to break projects down into smaller chunks.
- Teach him to organize projects and tackle the least appealing step first.
- Map out deadlines and set time limits for each step.
- Set up a reward system for completing a task.
- If needed, get tutors, outside help, or contact the school about the homework load.

**Why procrastinate?**

What makes kids procrastinate in the first place? If the classwork is too ho-hum, they get lazy and turned off to learning, educators say. Rote, mindless drills and worksheets breed boredom. So do uncreative teachers. When students' passions aren't nurtured, they become less interested in school. Other students lose interest if they lack confidence and don't think they'll do well at their work. When these students face academic obstacles, they withdraw.

They also withdraw when the work isn't appropriate for them, says Joan Newcomb, learning coordinator at The Little School in Bellevue, Washington. "The tasks they're asked to do should match their developmental stage," Newcomb explains. When students study subjects they choose and care about, they're "less likely to drag their feet," she says.

Often, adults expect too much from today's youngsters. "The amount of homework now considered necessary is a burden on most children," Newcomb says. All that pressure can backfire. "If a child makes it through a lot of work, but never wants to read another book in his life, no one has gained anything."

**What to do**

How do you handle kids who just can't seem to get things done?

Help them build the kinds of work habits that will carry them through school — and through life. Teach them that it's important to complete tasks that are given to them; then help them create work routines. O'Malley says it helps to break a project down into smaller chunks. "A student might look at the enormity of an assignment and not know where to start."

At The Learning Curve, instructors suggest students tackle the least appealing step of a project first. "Sometimes it's just a matter of gathering the research," says O'Malley. She also advises mapping out deadlines and setting time limits for each step. "That way, they know the 'torture' will only last, say, 30 minutes." Then set up a reward system, such as a short Internet hiatus, a five-minute telephone break, or simply time to relax.

Some kids lack organizational skills in areas such as taking notes, outlining, and highlighting, or need help in long-term planning.

If things still aren't going well, get outside help. That may mean talking to teachers about the workload itself or hiring private tutors. If you think the assignment is not appropriate, tell the school — and be clear about what you think is an unreasonable amount of homework.

Above all, help your children learn to feel good about themselves. Let them know you have confidence in them and in their ability to accept responsibility. Be a good example — show them how it's done. Maybe that closet will finally get organized.

CHAPTER 6

# Managing Social Issues

■ ■ ■ ■ ■

## SURVIVING THE SOCIAL SCENE

Have you ever watched preschoolers interact? They're happy to play with blocks, puzzles, dolls, games — whatever is available with whoever is available. It's a time of equal-opportunity socialization. These three- and four-year-olds haven't quite figured out the requisite boy/girl code of conduct, and "popularity" has yet to emerge as the preteen deity.

By grade school, those treasured days of social equanimity are pretty much over. "Let's play with blocks together" morphs into elaborate exercises in negotiation. "In early elementary school, friendship becomes more of an agreement and contract, with more expectations and rules," says Kathy Sarin, a school psychologist for the Bellevue School District in Washington. "Girls in particular will make up rules, such as 'You're going to be in charge of picking colors.' Then they practice negotiating what the specific rules will be."

As kids get older, their social world takes on greater significance. Kids spend twice as much time with their friends in later elementary years than they do in the early grades, and expectations become more sophisticated. "They begin to look for qualities such as loyalty, mutual understanding, and support from one another," Sarin says.

It may sound like great fun, but all that socializing comes at a price: Inevitably, kids get upset, hurt, or angry — or all of the above — because of problems that surface with their school friends. And that anger and disappointment can affect learning. Unhappy students can decide they "hate" school; some may even decide they don't want to attend at all. While some kids are naturally socially savvy and know how to read social cues, other kids just don't have those skills.

Peer relationships play a larger-than-life role in the day of a grade-school student. "A fifth-grader can cry for an hour if her friends have ganged up on her at recess," says Sarin.

Teachers and counselors say boys and girls deal with social issues differently. Deborah Phillips, founder of Coach-Parenting, which offers workshops and training for parents, says boys often use sports as a social measuring stick. Boys also score social points if they own cool things. "The most popular boy can be the one with the most 'toys' at home," says Phillips.

Girls are typically judged by who has the nicer clothes and who's involved in what activities. And they're subjected to the ever-present clique. That, as we know, can be ruthless. "Girls blackball each other during the year. There's behind-the-back chatter that girls use as a way to get ahead in the group," says Phillips.

## TIPS SURVIVING SOCIAL BUMPS

- Tell your child, "It has nothing to do with you." Someone who says mean things to another person does so based on how she is experiencing the world at that moment. Your child may even get to the point where she can feel sorry for someone who is feeling so badly about herself that she chooses to say mean things to other people.
- Expand your child's social circle through sports, clubs, and other activities with children from other schools or communities.
- Remember that a child who looks to only a small group of friends at school for reassurance about herself can experience big ups and downs in her self-esteem, depending on how those friends are treating her at any particular time.
- Help your child know who she is, so her sense of self is not dependent on comments made by others. You can do this in everyday situations by asking your child to stop and pay attention to herself and her thoughts.
- Ask your child to think about why she chooses to do something, about what is important to her right at that moment, or about what kind of person she is being at the moment.

Source: Coach-Parenting, *coach-parenting.com*

**Teach social skills**

How can you tell if your child is on the losing end of a social struggle? Kids who feel marginalized at school often become frustrated or withdrawn and are more likely to become aggressive, experts say. They might sleep less, cry more, become clingy, lose their appetites, and suffer from stomachaches or headaches.

When parents zero in on their child's social life as the source of his woes, they often reach for a quick fix. That might mean confronting other parents or the student who's making their kid miserable. But experts agree: It's better to help kids solve most minor social problems for themselves. Only if a child is experiencing a surfeit of teasing or bullying should parents approach a teacher or school counselor for help.

What else can parents do? They can suggest ways their kids can stand up for themselves. Consult Web sites and books, such as Stan Davis' *Schools Where Everyone Belongs,* to find positive ways to cope with teasing. Parents can also reinforce social skills by providing opportunities for their children to practice them. "Get kids involved in sports, church groups, and play dates. Plan activities that encourage interaction," Sarin suggests.

Parents should talk about qualities such as honesty and loyalty, and help kids understand why they are important. "The goal is not to make sure your children are never hurt by social dilemmas," Phillips says. "The goal is to help them understand how to make themselves OK again."

## Q & A WITH LAURA KASTNER, PH.D.

*Dr. Laura Kastner is associate professor of psychiatry and behavioral sciences at the University of Washington and the author, with writer Jennifer F. Wyatt, Ph.D., of* Getting to Calm: Cool-headed Strategies for Parenting Tweens and Teens.

**Q: How can you tell if your child is having social problems at school?**

You can't always! But sometimes children will complain about social difficulties directly, and other times their behavior may reflect it with sadness, acting out, bad dreams, loss of interest in school, or becoming noticeably isolated and friendless. So it is important to tune into your child's social world, so that you have information from your children, their friends' parents, and adults at school, in sports, or in other settings.

Research has shown that about 60 percent of children are popular or accepted, and another 20 percent are in a mixed category but not at risk. About 5 percent are children not chosen by others in their classes as preferred friends, but if they have at least one or two friends by the end of elementary school, they can be socially well-adjusted during middle school.

But that leaves 15 percent who are at risk. These kids may feel lonely and be at risk for being teased, bullied, or rejected, or turn into bullies themselves. These are the children to whom parents need to attend before harm is done.

**Q: How do parents know what is normal social interaction and what is tormenting or bullying behavior?**

There is a large spectrum of social interaction, which includes positive characteristics such as thoughtfulness, inclusion, and friendliness at one end and rejection, exclusion, teasing, and bullying at the other. Most kids demonstrate a lot of positive social behaviors, because these qualities are valued and modeled in their families and cultures, but most children will also explore the use of power in their peers' lives and be cruel on occasion as well.

There are relatively few classic bullies like the ones dramatized in books and movies, like the big, sadistic guy who relentlessly torments innocent victims. But bullies exist in subtler forms and they have a strong need to dominate, threaten, or harass others with an intention to hurt, intimidate, or humiliate. Much more common are the negative leaders in a class, who tease a lot at their best and may bully at their worst, especially with the help of a group that eggs them on. And even more common are the bystanders, who are covertly supporting the whole process.

Parents need to know that almost all children are mean on occasion and that it takes a long time to "refine" and socialize some of their baser instincts. Although we want to take a stand on our values about kindness, inclusion, and sticking up for the good, we also need to realize that social dynamics among children are very complicated — with many negative peer interactions happening without a clear victim and villain.

**Q: Is all teasing harmful?**

Playful teasing can be fun and part of a friendly exchange, and you know it's the good kind when everyone smiles and feels good about it. By contrast, hurtful teasing includes put-downs, name calling, mild humiliation, and irritating statements that are meant to make someone feel uncomfortable. There is an enormous amount of aggressive humor used to put people down — more than most people acknowledge. Just like physical assaults, verbal assaults represent ways to express aggression, establish superiority, discharge discomfort, and command prowess with others. However, ask children about their making aggressive statements like "You're so gay" or "I can't believe you're wearing THAT," and they will virtually always say, "I was just kidding!"

We need to promote empathy, the Golden Rule, and gaining perspective ("How would you feel?") whenever we can, but avoid the "shame/blame" trap that turns us into lecturers and Pollyannas. Walking this line is hard, but parents need to be aware that aggressive teasing is on the continuum of social cruelty.

**Q: What is the fallout of being the victim of bullying or teasing?**

Parents frequently compare the relative harm of how boys versus girls express social aggression. Whether it is the constant, nasty, and direct put-downs of boys, or the indirect rumoring, gossiping, exclusion, or outright lies spread by girls, the long-term damage of social cruelty can accompany individuals into their adulthoods. Children who are victims of bullying can end up depressed and lose whole chunks of their childhoods when they need to be developing social skills, trust in others, and interpersonal problem-solving. Also, rejected children can become bullies as a way of dealing with their anger, depression, and despair.

**Q: What are the dangers of being the person who is taunting or bullying others?**

The dangers can be as subtle as incorporating mean-spiritedness and a lack of empathy into adulthood relationships or as catastrophic as carrying out heinous crimes on others. Since bullies receive reinforcement for their behavior by gaining power and by the attention they receive from tormenting others, they are likely to repeat the behavior unless strong measures are taken to stop it. Intervention by parents, peers, and schools is needed to interrupt this pattern.

**Q: Should a parent confront another parent if they think their child is being picked on?**

First, the parents need to size up the situation and figure out if the child is reporting on the slings and arrows of a typical, messy social life with peers, or it's something that requires adult intervention. Important factors to consider are the child's age, temperament, social skill level, and the circumstances of the "picking."

If it is typical mild teasing, parents might want to help their own child cope with the predicament. Parents can coach their kids on strategies for responding to teasing, like a humorous rejoinder (e.g., "I know! I can't believe how many freckles I have either!"), a compliment (e.g., "I love your complexion"), or a deflection (e.g., "Freckles aren't my problem — it's my dog. He isn't housebroken. Do you know how bad our kitchen stinks?"). If there is a problematic pattern of aggressive teasing from a friend, parents may want to talk with that friend's parents, but only if there is reason to believe that the child has already tried to reverse the pattern and/or that the parental meeting can be constructive. If it sounds like a matter of bullying at school, parents should contact the school and insist on intervention.

**Q: How can parents teach and reinforce values to their children that will help them be more accepting of their peers?**

Parents need to make their children aware of the subtleties of social cruelty. Talk about the moral responsibility of bystanders to confront a bully. Give examples of "hero" behaviors, be they in an employment situation (whistle-blowers), novels (the kid who sticks up for the underdog), or movies (the nonviolent versions of heroes need to be emphasized!).

There is almost always a pecking order in peer systems, with attractive, popular kids and athletes at the top of the hierarchy. A subtle way to broaden the perspectives of children is to openly admire peers who reflect other values, such as creativity, thoughtfulness, loyalty, resilience, generosity, and modesty — especially when those peers happen to be from a different ethnic or socio-economic background, are suffering from a chronic illness, or are struggling with special challenges.

**Q: What can a parent do if their child is simply being "left out"? Is this necessarily a bad thing?**

Being left out of social activities is one of those typical hard things of childhood and adolescence. It's inevitable, and can even be productive when the child regroups and retools, and figures out how to make "lemonade out of lemons." Resilience develops from coping with common adversities.

If the exclusion is becoming a pattern, it is acceptable for parents to try being a social engineer, if it is OK with the child and not taking the form of "buying a friendship." When a child is "between friends," it is also fine to sign them up for some activities, since this will keep them active (not moping), potentially provide a new friendship source, and maybe even produce a new hobby!

## IS YOUR CHILD A BULLY?

Admit it. In the back of your mind, tucked in with anxiety about whether your child will ace his math exam or be chosen for the tennis team, lurks something you fear, maybe most of all: Will your kid get picked on? Left out? Pushed, shoved, or taunted?

No one wants their child to be bullied. And few kids sail through school without living through some form of mean-kid victimization, especially in today's cyberspace world. Maybe someone started an IM rumor about your daughter or posted cringe-worthy shots of your son on Facebook.

But here's a jarring thought: What if it's your child who is doing the bullying? What if your daughter is the mean girl who's excluding kids from the lunchroom clique? Or your son is humiliating other boys by calling them names and shoving them around on the basketball court?

Sometimes parents, unwilling to believe their child is the class tormentor, react with disbelief when someone suggests their perfect little girl is teasing the heck out of the other children, says Peter Sheras, Ph.D., psychology professor at the University of Virginia and author of the book *Your Child: Bully or Victim?* "How do you say to parents, 'I'm worried your child is a bully' without them saying, 'Talk to my lawyer'?"

Bullies can be hard to spot, because they're likely to dial up the charm when around adults, experts point out. Often street-smart and socially savvy, they realize bullying others is an easy path to social status.

"It's all about power," says Bridgid Normand, senior program developer for Committee for Children. "Kids who bully others are after dominance. They are often the popular ones, the kids who are throwing their weight around in the schools."

And in case you're thinking it's better to bully than be bullied, think again. The long-term outcomes for bullies who don't change their behavior are dismal, Normand says. "When kids develop a pattern of aggression, it tends to continue and surface later in dating, family, and workplace relationships."

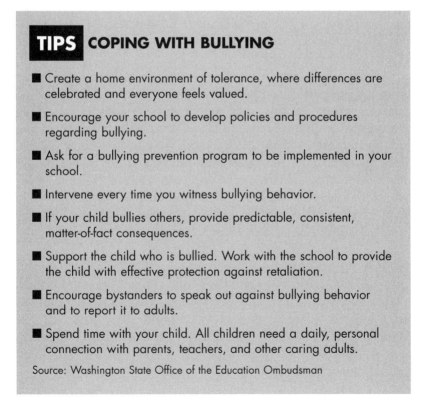

## TIPS COPING WITH BULLYING

- Create a home environment of tolerance, where differences are celebrated and everyone feels valued.
- Encourage your school to develop policies and procedures regarding bullying.
- Ask for a bullying prevention program to be implemented in your school.
- Intervene every time you witness bullying behavior.
- If your child bullies others, provide predictable, consistent, matter-of-fact consequences.
- Support the child who is bullied. Work with the school to provide the child with effective protection against retaliation.
- Encourage bystanders to speak out against bullying behavior and to report it to adults.
- Spend time with your child. All children need a daily, personal connection with parents, teachers, and other caring adults.

Source: Washington State Office of the Education Ombudsman

**Natural-born bully?**

So, what makes kids bully? Will scientists one day come up with some kind of genetic marker for bullying? Is it in our DNA?

Not likely. "Bullying is a learned phenomenon that has to do with social pressure," says Sheras. Some kids turn to bullying — or ally themselves with bullies — to avoid being victims themselves, he says. "It's easier to hang out with the bully than to risk the finger being pointed at you."

Bullies harbor an excess of anger and tend to see the world in black and white. "They feel the world has treated them unfairly; that they don't get enough acknowledgment for what they do," Sheras says. "They're opinionated and judgmental."

Bullying can surface as early as elementary school when a group of kids decides, "We don't like Emily anymore." The behavior, experts agree, peaks in middle school, when the peer group becomes omnipotent. "There's a need to establish dominance and social status," says Normand. "Some kids try to be trendsetters, telling others to wear this or listen to that kind of music. They often target kids who have less status."

By high school, power plays emerge when students marginalize other kids they find less desirable, leaving them on the fringe of social activities. "As kids get older, the behavior goes from obvious and typical to subtle and manipulative," says Mike Donlin, a senior program consultant with Seattle Public Schools.

Contrary to popular stereotypes, bullying is not a "kid thing" that evaporates as children grow up, says Donlin. "The negative behaviors just evolve as kids get more sophisticated," he says. "It turns into hazing, sexual harassment, aggression, and cyberbullying — all variations on the same thing."

**What to do**

How can you tell if your child is a bully? Watch how your child treats other kids, experts advise. Monitor electronic communications and pay attention to social-networking Web sites, such as MySpace and Facebook. "Notice who your child hangs out with," says Sheras. "Does he spend time with a tough crowd? Do other kids shy away from him?"

Let's say your kid is one of those super-socially adept kids who has you — and the grownups around you — successfully seduced. Everyone (especially you!) sees this child as a charismatic leader. Then, one day, you get a call from school. It turns out that your child has been belittling other kids. "The most important thing to do is stay calm," says Normand. "Really listen to what the teachers are telling you and don't get defensive." Then begin working with the teacher, administrators, and counselors to find out what's going on.

If the negative behavior doesn't stop, consult a mental-health professional, she advises. "You want to nip this in the bud."

Other red flags to watch for? Bullies often like to dominate others, hide their behavior from adults, blame someone else for their problems, and derive satisfaction from the fear or pain of others, says Normand. "They lack concern for the feelings of other people. It's a piece of empathy they just don't get."

If you see a pattern like this beginning to emerge, take action. If you overhear your daughter chatting away on the telephone, spreading nasty rumors and gossiping about a classmate, take away phone privileges. "Tell your child, 'If you're not able to manage yourself, my job as a parent is to step in and manage things for you,'" suggests Normand.

And point out the negative behavior, she says. "Say, 'I heard what you were saying and that's bullying behavior. It is not OK to treat people that way.'"

## HOW GENDER AFFECTS LEARNING

This may be hard to believe today, but not too long ago, parents viewed their newborns as blank slates upon which virtually everything — including gender identity — could be imprinted. Little boys preferred trucks, and little girls preferred dolls, said the experts, only because those are the toys their moms and dads gave them.

How long we '80s parents bought into that message depended upon which came first: watching real-life boys and girls up close or absorbing the most up-to-date research in brain science.

With apologies to Marlo Thomas and her iconic album, *Free to Be You and Me*, most of us discovered quickly enough that — surprise! — boys and girls are different. As Seattle child psychiatrist Diane Stein notes, "Yes, some girls played with trucks, some boys played with dolls. But then the girls figured out they could make truck families."

In his book *Boys and Girls Learn Differently!*, Michael Gurian highlights the latest findings in neuroscience and explains the way brain-based differences affect boys and girls.

The evidence, he finds, reinforces what parents and teachers commonly observe in elementary-school classrooms: Female brains mature faster than male brains; girls communicate better verbally than boys; boys are more spatial; girls tend to be social; and boys tend to "manage social energy through dominance or pecking order."

But Stein cautions against drawing clear gender distinctions across the board. "Beware of generalizations," she says. "There's a large spectrum within the category of boys and girls. There's also more overlap within each group than differences."

In other words, look closely and you'll find girls who like to climb trees and play pick-up basketball, and boys who choose fantasy play over roughhousing. If you stick with stereotype, you ignore the individual.

And while today's theorists seem to favor nature in the never-ending cultural and scientific nature-versus-nurture debate, don't underestimate the effect of a child's environment, Stein says. "I don't think parents realize the extent to which they emphasize or reinforce certain kinds of gender behavior."

For example, aggression is much less tolerated in girls than in boys, she says. "We do so much of this reflexively," she says. "Parents and teachers need to be honest with themselves and be aware of this."

### Alike — except when they're not

Whenever Susan Small hears people talk about brain chemistry and male and female traits, she takes it with a grain of salt. Small, director of a Seattle-area tutoring company, tells parents to consider every child unique. Yet, she acknowledges, "some things do stand out."

Girls, she notes, don't like getting into trouble, and boys seem to accept it more; girls stand back and figure out the rules, and boys are more aggressive about exploring their world; girls communicate with detail, and boys communicate quite well with one or two words.

How do these differences show up in the elementary-school classroom? Boys can be more global, says Small. "They see that big-picture thing, but they can miss the details." Girls, she contends, often pay attention to the details.

And boys don't particularly like to elaborate, a characteristic that might work to their disadvantage when writing an essay.

Once they identify their sons' or daughters' individual strengths and weaknesses, parents can help build their children's skills in areas that need a boost, Small says.

"The boy who gives a one-word response might need some coaching," she says. Discuss with him the reasons why elaborating in his written work might be important. Then offer him tools that will help him learn to use description, she suggests. "Tell him to think of categories such as size, color, and emotion. If he's describing a dog, ask him: 'Is the dog happy or sad?'"

Your daughter, she says, might write "more than you need to know." She needs to learn to edit. "Ask her to tell you the most salient point. Teach her to narrow down and highlight the important parts of her essay."

Parents should also pay attention to what's going on at school. How do teachers relate to the students? Are they aware of male/female brain differences and current research on the brain and gender? And most important: Are they teaching to boys and girls, and not just to a generic bunch of kids? That, the experts say, is how every teacher should approach every class.

## TIPS SUPPORTING GENDER DIFFERENCES IN LEARNING

- Understand that there are differences between male and female brains, but don't generalize or stereotype — there are overlaps within each group.
- Be aware of the way you reinforce certain kinds of gender behavior.
- Help your son use description in his written work.
- Help your daughter learn to edit.
- Pay attention to what is going on in your child's classroom and the way the teacher relates to both boys and girls.

## Q & A WITH MICHAEL THOMPSON, PH.D.

*Michael Thompson is a psychologist, consultant, and the author/co-author of eight books, including* Raising Cain: Protecting the Emotional Life of Boys.

**Q: The experts tell us that boys' and girls' brains differ. Should that affect the way parents raise and relate to their children?**

Yes. Neuroscientific researchers now tell us that there are significant differences between the brains of men and women. Steven Pinker, a professor at Harvard, writes that neuro-imaging techniques and other new technologies for observing the brain have produced 60 different studies revealing meaningful differences in the brain function of the two genders. But we do not yet know how to translate those findings into specific recommendations for child-rearing.

We know that children are all more human than they are gendered; that is, they need love, nurturance, guidance, limits, and discipline, whether they are boys or girls. We know that there are enormous variations in personality and temperament; that is, there are quiet, nonathletic boys and risk-taking, athletic girls. It is more important that parents respond to the personality characteristics of their children than to treat them in a "boy" way or a "girl" way.

**Q: In what ways do boys and girls develop differently?**

Girls, on average, pick up language faster than boys, and boys, on average, are more physically active, more impulsive, and developmentally immature in comparison to girls of the same chronological age. Seventh-grade girls sum this all up by contemptuously saying, "Boys are so immature!" What they mean, and what science tells us, is that boys have a different arc of development than girls.

We've known that, physically, girls usually stop growing in height when they get their first period; boys continue growing in height up until the age of 19 or 20, but it is also true psychologically. Boys take longer to mature. That said, boys' development is still trustworthy. They do get there. They do grow into hardworking men and responsible fathers.

**Q: Why do we hear that schools these days are "failing boys"? What does that mean?**

Girls are outperforming boys in schools today. More girls finish high school; more boys drop out. Today, 58 percent of college degrees are going to young women; 56 percent of graduate degrees are going to young women. Once we removed the real and psychological barriers to girls getting educations, they zoomed past boys. They do as well in math and science as boys do, but are much further ahead in reading and writing.

**Q: In what fundamental ways do boys learn differently than girls?**

There is no simple answer to this question. Some girls struggle to learn; some boys learn very easily. There are many, many factors at work here that influence learning: IQ, family background, education of parents, type of school, quality of teaching, etc. The one thing we can say for sure is that there is more brain variability in boys than there is in girls, so that more boys find the conventional classroom challenging.

**Q: Girls seem to outpace boys in the early grades. Why does this happen?**

The elementary-school classroom is four-fifths language based, and girls, on average, are better at language than boys. They have better fine motor skills, so their handwriting is more legible and it's easier for them to write. The elementary classroom seems to favor girl strengths and it hits boys in their areas of weakness: sitting still and listening to adults talk.

**Q: What can parents do to help their sons succeed in school?**

Two suggestions, only one of which relates to school: If you want your son to do well in school, create an academic atmosphere at home on school evenings; the rest of the time, show your son what your education means to you. When your son has homework assigned, don't do it for him, don't check it obsessively, but after dinner sit down with a book or a newspaper near where he is working to model. In non-homework times (and that's most of the time), your family should play board games, word games, sing songs in the car, listen to books on tape, and attend concerts and the theater. And read to your son at bedtime.

**Q: How can they help their daughters?**

All of the above suggestions apply to daughters, too. If you have a perfectionistic, driven daughter who can't *not* do her homework and who stresses out about it, make sure she gets to bed at a decent hour and gets a good night's sleep.

## PUPPY LOVE: YOUR CHILD'S FIRST CRUSH

It's not easy to be young and in love; ask any preteen girl. Most likely, she's obsessing right now over a boy in her class — a boy who thinks having a girlfriend is cool, but is frankly more interested in who'll be playing basketball with him after school.

The gender gap's only one of the hurdles that kids — and their parents — face when they embark on those early relationships grownups like to call "crushes."

For most kids, it begins around fifth or sixth grade, though some precocious children will start having crushes as young as second grade. A new gender awareness begins to emerge at this age. "Kids start hanging out more with kids of their own sex," explains Piper Sangston, a social worker at Chinook Middle School in Bellevue, Washington. "They don't want to be teased about 'liking' someone."

By seventh grade, schools introduce sex ed, kids show up at school dances, and sparks start to fly. "Things become more complicated," says Sangston. "Girls have to be prettier and nicer. They have more girl-girl problems because they start to compete for boys."

Girls, vying for the same boys, sometimes betray each other, and best-friend relationships can suffer, Sangston says.

Some girls become obsessive. "They call the boy they like 12 times a day, or write him multiple messages, or create fantasies about him," says Bill Meleney, a Tacoma, Washington, family therapist. It doesn't help that 13-year-old girls are considered "culturally incomplete" without a boyfriend, he says.

What are the boys doing amid all this chaos? Most likely, downloading the latest from iTunes or playing the hottest Xbox game. Boys tend to be more casual about all this, says Meleney. "If a guy likes a girl, it's because she's cool — or because he's trying to get into sex too early, to prove something."

He may try to prove something, even if he hasn't had sex. "Preadolescent boys can begin to get this macho hypersexual attitude," says Janine Jones, Ph.D., a University of Washington child psychologist. "They will talk like they are doing things when, in fact, they're not."

That's when a father — or a strong male role model — needs to become involved, she says. "These boys need to learn what's appropriate and what's not."

### Stay connected

Young love has been around for a long time, but Twitter, Facebook, and YouTube have not. Thanks to the Internet, boy-girl relationships move at a hypersonic pace these days. "It's a speedier rumor mill than 20 years ago," says Sangston. "The information is faster, so the relationships are faster."

And anything goes. "Everything's talked about over the Internet," she says. "There are no rules. And it's easy to be mean." That's why a very old game must be monitored in a very new way. More than ever, mom and dad (or other caretakers) need to be firmly plugged into their kids' lives. "Parents should ask their kids a lot of questions," says Meleney. "They should have their kids' friends over for dinner. They should meet the friends' parents."

They should also respect their child's privacy — up to a point. That point is the computer and the cell phone. "That's where kids have no right to absolute privacy," Meleney contends. Meleney keeps track of his son's social networking passwords, and checks out his email and cell-phone bills. "This," he says, "is not negotiable."

#### TIPS STAYING CLUED INTO YOUR CHILD'S FIRST CRUSH

- Keep your eye on your child's computer use.
- Watch for red flags, such as a sudden drop in grades or obsession with seeing a friend.
- Watch for behavioral changes, such as extreme secretiveness.
- Be more open about your own first relationships.
- Be available to talk to (not lecture!) your child.

**Watch for red flags**

At the preteen or early-teen stage, "relationship" is often code for "hanging out." And it shouldn't be much more than that. But what if it is? What if it's way more than that? And how's a parent to figure that out?

Keep your eye out for certain red flags, says Jones. A sudden drop in grades is one. Obsession with seeing, calling, or emailing the friend is another. "If a child is so preoccupied with a girlfriend or boyfriend that he or she stops doing homework or is texting too much, that's cause for concern," says Jones.

And a parent's antennae should be buzzing if a child is overly secretive. "This is the kid who closes Facebook when the parent enters the room, or gets defensive when asked about school," she says.

So, how can you cultivate honesty in your child? Model it, says Miriam Hirschstein, Ph.D., a research scientist for Committee for Children. "You can afford to be a little more open about your own experiences. What was it like for you with your first relationships?"

Use humor, she says. "Tell stories on yourself. Honor their dignity."

Be willing to talk and joke, not just demand or lecture, says Meleney. "Kids who think their parents actually like and respect them and who know what the boundaries are will be much happier and well adjusted, and more open to communicating."

CHAPTER 7

# Advocating for Your Child

■ ■ ■ ■ ■

## LEARNING THROUGH PLAY

The country became enamored with academics around the time the Russians spun *Sputnik* into space. That was 1957, and kids in the United States began studying math and science with new vigor. A decade later, the government introduced Head Start, a preschool program aimed at preparing disadvantaged children for school.

Education reform went into full gear in 1983, when President Reagan's National Commission on Excellence in Education came out with "A Nation at Risk," a report that found that a "rising tide of mediocrity" threatened America's public school system.

Fast-forward to the next century and you're looking at a whole new world of educational expectations. They trickle down from the No Child Left Behind–driven Department of Education to the crazily competitive college-admission process, to the ever-present standardized testing, to real letters-and-numbers learning for the littlest students.

Where do those expectations end up? Most likely, at your front door. If you find yourself drilling your three-year-old on his ABCs because you're worried he won't hold his own when he starts school, you're not alone. After all, isn't kindergarten the new first grade?

It's no wonder leading psychologists and educators in this country, fed up with what they see as a misguided push for early academics, are demanding we let kids be kids.

### The push for play

The Alliance for Childhood, an organization based in Maryland, would like to see schools offer more play and less testing. Alliance backers feel that all the cerebral intensity overwhelms kids and contributes to later behavior and learning problems. The Alliance for Childhood movement is gaining traction. Child-advocate superstars such as T. Berry Brazelton, David Elkind, and Daniel Goleman publicly support its agenda. The media is getting on board, too: A 2007 *Newsweek* cover posed the question "Are Kids Getting Pushed Too Fast, Too Soon?"

Yet research coming out of topnotch facilities such as the University of Washington's I-LABS shows that very young children — even newborns — learn more quickly and efficiently than adults.

I-LABS codirectors Patricia Kuhl and Andrew Meltzoff wrote *The Scientist in the Crib: Minds, Brains, and How Children Learn*, a research-based book that advocates very early learning. In fact, the Baby Einstein, earlier-is-better culture has virtually exploded in the last decade with learning ops for tots: lessons in Mandarin; classes in math and literacy; Leapster tech toys that teach subtraction and phonics.

"Parents are concerned and fearful about their kids' future," says Joan Almon, chair of the Alliance for Childhood. "They think their children need to start things as early as possible if they are going to make it in the world."

## TIPS ENCOURAGING PLAY

- Provide art opportunities. Let kids initiate their own drawings.
- Encourage make-believe play. It's a way for children to try on roles and work through what's going on in their lives.
- Let them play with other kids. They feel safe trying out language with their friends.
- Schedule unstructured play. Let the kids choose their own activities.
- Give children simple materials, such as crayons, paper, toy logs, and clay to play with.
- Read to them and ask them to make up an ending to a story or draw a character. Make it an interactive activity.
- Play rhyming games.
- Tell stories that aren't in books. Children develop a different way of listening that way.

Today's kindergarteners face an excessively amped-up curriculum, she says. In the old days, expectations were minimal: You turned five, you showed up. "Now, parents and teachers have to prepare their three- and four-year-olds for kindergarten entry," Almon says. "Many children are not developmentally ready for this."

In the race to meet test standards and boost brain power, educators are neglecting to make time for old-fashioned fun and creativity, says Dorothy Singer, a Yale University professor and author of *Play = Learning*. "Teachers are under pressure and teaching in a mechanical, rote way. We're seeing kids who know they have to prepare for the tests — and are depressed, anxious, and on medication."

There's little upside to learning the alphabet at age two, says Almon. "Why does everything have to be at a top, top level? Those parents who are so proud of their child knowing his letters should ask, 'How does my child play? Is his imagination kicking in?'"

Some claim the No Child Left Behind Act has muffled playtime. Under that federal act, all students in grades three through eight are tested yearly in math and reading, with each state setting its own learning benchmarks. "As [former] President Bush says, 'What gets measured gets done,'" says Rebecca Neale, spokeswoman for the U.S. Department of Education. The hope, she says, is that teachers will use innovative methods to bring students up to grade level in math and reading. The goal? To ensure American kids will emerge as world leaders in technological innovation and science.

### Standards step up

Judging from a recent study released by the American Institutes for Research, we've got a long way to go. Comparing standardized test scores of eighth-grade students in the United States with those of their peers abroad, the study found students in Singapore, South Korea, and Japan outperform students even in high-scoring states, such as Massachusetts.

That's the kind of evidence that has the Department of Education on edge — and has states revising their math standards.

Preschools pay close attention to elevated expectations and adjust their programs to fit their school districts' standards. Debra Gibbons, director of Little Gems Preschool, with locations near Seattle, raised the learning benchmarks in her classes after neighboring school districts upped their kindergarten benchmarks. Instead of merely mastering letters and sounds, Little Gems kids learn words by sight and write books. They also play counting games and practice patterning and graphing. "I try to offer a fun, playful curriculum; the kids don't even know they're learning," says Gibbons.

So what's it going to be: Work or play? Leapster or leapfrog?

Perhaps a little of each. There are ways parents can play with their child and support their learning.

"It's a false choice to think you must decide between creativity and academic rigor," says Eric Liu, an author and educator who serves on the Washington State Board of Education. "Play can be purposeful. You can teach someone the basics through creativity."

Never underestimate the power of imagination, he says. "People who get the cool jobs are ones who exercise their creative muscles. Where would Microsoft or the biotech business be without creativity? Schools can meet benchmarks without letting the 'test' be the point. We need to trust principals and teachers more in helping kids reach standards in flexible and innovative ways."

Those ways can be as simple as providing kids with a set of blocks or as easy as piecing together a "house corner." That's what Seattle-area teacher Linda Arland does in her kindergarten class. The popular play area includes a kitchen, a basket of stuffed animals, dress-up clothes, baby dolls, and a cash register. "The dramatic role-playing that happens there offers a natural arena for children to practice language and social skills," she says.

## Q & A WITH JOAN ALMON

*Joan Almon is the chair of the Alliance for Childhood, a national organization that promotes policies and practices supporting child-initiated imaginative play and the love of learning.*

**Q: How does play promote learning?**

In authentic, child-initiated, and child-directed play, children encounter many challenges, beginning with the decision of what they want to play. Should they build a house, a fort, a hospital, a rocket? What do their playmates want? How do they sort out the differences? Along the way, they learn lesson after lesson, such as knowing their own minds and what matters to them at the moment, while also knowing what their friends want and how to negotiate for compromise or joint ventures. They learn how to use the resources at hand to build what they want and how to sustain play ideas and let them evolve over time, sometimes over many days and weeks.

**Q: What are some ways young children can learn through play?**

Physically, children challenge themselves in play and develop physical skills such as dexterity, balance, strength, and flexibility in movement. For children, play is the natural form of exercise, and they can remain busy in play all day long, whether they are playing with small items and developing finger skills, or building forts and climbing trees.

Socially, children master the art of being with others in play. They learn to make rules and change rules, and in the process, to negotiate all kinds of situations. In role-playing, they explore all kinds of roles and life situations with others. They play out birth and death, and everything in between.

Emotionally, children use play to work through all kinds of situations, some of them painful or frightening. It's been shown that children under stress can use play to reduce their stress levels. Unfortunately, today's children have more and more stress in their lives, and less and less opportunity to alleviate the stress through play.

**Q: Is it harmful to encourage very young children to read or do number problems?**

Most young children who are inwardly ready to master reading, writing, or number problems will show signs of interest. I've always suggested to parents of four- to six-year-olds that they respond to their children's questions, but not push more on them than the child is asking for. Many five-year-olds, for instance, show intense interest in math or writing and reading for a few weeks. Then the interest fades away until first grade, when it returns strongly — if they haven't burnt out on too early a focus.

Preschool- and kindergarten-age children are generally not ready for consistent day-in, day-out structured teaching of literacy and numeracy. One can characterize their interest in being taught literacy and numeracy as "a little bit goes a long way."

**Q: Are there repercussions from this kind of emphasis on starting early?**

There is a growing amount of stress and anger in young children, and while there are probably many causes, one that is frequently cited is the unrealistic goal of teaching reading and numeracy to children between the ages of three and six. We hear of kindergarten rage, where children have extreme outbursts in kindergarten and are likely to hurt others. Many educators feel that young children are being asked to function in ways better suited for first-graders, and that many cannot bear the stress of the situation.

Many teachers complain that children show signs of burnout by the time they are in third or fourth grade. It seems that demanding too much academic achievement too soon backfires, and the children lose interest in learning by age nine or ten.

**Q: Why is there an increased focus on academics in younger and younger kids?**

The pressure for this approach comes from two directions. One is that parents often want to be assured that their children are getting an advanced approach to learning so they will get ahead in life.

The other pressure comes in response to a real need, which is to find a way to overcome the gap in school success between low-income children and others. It has been argued for years that low-income preschool children need an intense focus on literacy and numeracy instruction if they are to catch up with middle-class children. The gap is real, and early intervention is needed, but so far there is little evidence of long-term gains for low-income children who are given early childhood classes that are highly structured with teacher-led instruction. While such approaches can lead to gains in first and second grade, the gains tend to fade out after that.

**Q: We know that children's brains are capable of learning and processing information very early. How do we help kids maximize those opportunities?**

The child's brain is open to all forms of sense impressions and life experiences. Most young children have an enormous inner urge to connect with the world and learn all they can about it, but they want to do that in their own way and on their own terms. They need the secure base of warm, caring relationships, and then they are ready to learn. By giving children a rich environment with lots of open-ended play materials (in contrast to defined toys), coupled with other healthy essentials — including music, art, and rich language experiences, and gardening, cooking, and other hands-on experiences — they will tend to explore every facet of life and make it their own.

Starting in first grade, there is a shift in most children, and they are eager to be "taught" by a respected teacher. But before that, most will learn much more through self-discovery and play. The wise teacher or parent knows how to create a simple but rich environment for learning and also how to set an example as an active learner/worker. The child imitates the adult and is supported in this process by the rich activities of the environment.

**Q: Why is it important to help kids develop creative thinking?**
Young children's minds are naturally creative and inventive. They do not tend to think in linear, rational ways, but in lateral, idiosyncratic ways. One speaks of the "magical thinking" of young children.

Gradually, by age six or seven, children's thinking becomes more concrete and rational, and eventually, in puberty, it also becomes quite abstract. Yet the spark of creativity remains so that their mature thinking is still capable of developing new, innovative ideas. Without the creative mind, life becomes very dull, and little headway can be made culturally. Creativity and innovation are needed to meet the challenges of life, and the creative mind is one of the great gifts of life.

## MAKING THE MOST OF PARENT-TEACHER RELATIONSHIPS

Mimi Tang wants parents to view learning as a team effort. For education to work well, "everyone must participate," says Tang, an elementary-school teacher in Portland, Oregon.

Her observation is echoed by many of today's educators, who point to "collaboration" as academia's latest buzzword. "It's about building the community of learning," Tang says. "The teacher is the leader, but the parent is also involved in the relationship. This is a democratic process."

Parents should find a communication approach that works for them and for their child's teacher — and then stick with it. Educators want parents and caretakers involved, alert, and aware of what's going on in the classroom.

And they should do it all without coming on too strong.

The parent-teacher relationship is a curious one. If parents hang back, they're labeled disinterested. But over-the-top, ever-present folks are every teacher's bad dream. No one appreciates the mom or dad who has a better idea of how to teach the class — and shares it with the instructor. What do teachers like? They welcome parents who make an effort to learn and reinforce what's happening in their children's school.

## TIPS BUILDING AN EFFECTIVE PARENT-TEACHER RELATIONSHIP

- Ask the teacher how he or she likes to communicate. Find out how to maintain contact without disrupting your child's class.
- Recognize that your own school experiences color the way you view your child's.
- Realize that your child is not the only student the teacher is thinking about.
- If there is a problem, contact the teacher soon, so that a timely solution can be found.
- Respect the teacher's instructional time. That means avoiding what principal Gary Tubbs calls "the fly-by conference on the way to getting your latte."
- Don't go over the teacher's head. Start with the teacher; if things don't get better, then go to the principal.
- Stay in touch. It's more essential than ever that parents and teachers work in partnership.
- Be nice! If you are warm and friendly, chances are your child's teacher will be more receptive.

### The new parent-teacher relationship

Face it: The days when parents simply shuttled their children to school, signed the report card, and exchanged pleasantries with the teacher at open house are long gone. Today's catchphrase seems to be "We're in this together."

What's changed? The way parents view their children's teachers, for starters. People often live farther from their families; with little or no support system nearby, they rely on teachers. "Who else do you look to for parenting advice?" asks Tang.

Often, parents look to Tang. Questions range from "What time should my daughter go to bed at night?" to "How do I say 'no' to my son?"

"Teachers become important advocates in the journey of child-rearing," she says. "Sometimes, parents just want their hands held. But most often, what they really need to know is 'Is my child normal?'"

Gary Tubbs views the parent-teacher connection as a critical partnership. "We are a diverse population," says Tubbs, founding principal of The New School at South Shore in Seattle. "There are different kinds of cultures, different learning styles, different backgrounds. We have to be very open to learning about kids from parents."

That's one reason the school's staff works to keep parents involved through home visits and parenting classes. "Being inclusive is part of the philosophy of the school," Tubbs says. "We try to operate from our heart."

## DOES YOUR CHILD HAVE A LEARNING DISABILITY?

Wouldn't it be great if all kids could learn math, reading, and writing seamlessly, with just the right amount of effort in just the appropriate amount of time? It would certainly make a teacher's job easier.

But the reality is that every child learns differently. Some learn visually, some spatially, some learn best by listening.

For another subset of children, learning is much more difficult. These kids aren't simply coping with assorted study styles. They have problems processing data that make it harder to grasp academic subjects. Educators call these kids "learning disabled."

According to the National Center for Learning Disabilities, or NCLD, a learning disability is a "neurological disorder that affects the brain's ability to receive, process, store, and respond to information." About 5 percent of all children in public schools in this country — that's 2.8 million kids — have a learning disability, according to the NCLD.

Does your child have a learning disability? Figuring that out isn't always easy. Some learning-disabled kids experience speech and language difficulties; others have problems learning to read or using fine motor skills. "Learning disabilities can be difficult to diagnose before children are in first grade," says Elizabeth MacKenzie, Ph.D., a Seattle-area child and adolescent psychologist. "With very bright kids, it's even harder to diagnose early."

### Helping every child learn

Children with a learning disability generally have average or above average intelligence, according to the NCLD. And while kids with autism and attention deficit hyperactivity disorder, or ADHD, may also have specific learning disabilities, autism and ADHD are considered separate disorders.

In 2004, the U.S. Department of Education redefined "specific learning disability" to include "the imperfect ability" to listen, think, speak, read, write, spell, or do mathematical calculations.

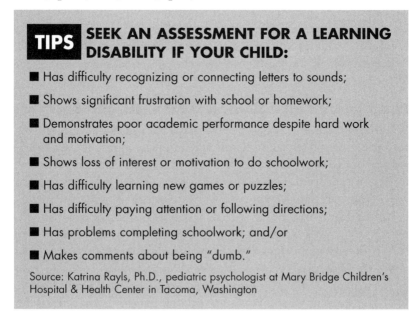

**TIPS** **SEEK AN ASSESSMENT FOR A LEARNING DISABILITY IF YOUR CHILD:**

- Has difficulty recognizing or connecting letters to sounds;
- Shows significant frustration with school or homework;
- Demonstrates poor academic performance despite hard work and motivation;
- Shows loss of interest or motivation to do schoolwork;
- Has difficulty learning new games or puzzles;
- Has difficulty paying attention or following directions;
- Has problems completing schoolwork; and/or
- Makes comments about being "dumb."

Source: Katrina Rayls, Ph.D., pediatric psychologist at Mary Bridge Children's Hospital & Health Center in Tacoma, Washington

That's not all educators have redefined. According to Sheldon Horowitz, Ed.D., director of professional services at the NCLD, pretty much everything has changed lately in the world of learning disabilities. "Schools have become much better at knowing that a learning disability is not something that precludes a child from having high levels of success," says Horowitz. "The message that's gotten through is, while a learning disability is a learning challenge, it need not result in failure."

In the old days, learning-disabled students would get extra help in school pullout programs. "The kids would go out to their special classes, then return to their social studies class, and crash and burn," says Horowitz. "The general-education teachers were not familiar with what was needed to make these kids successful."

These days, schools work to help every child learn — including kids with a learning disability. A good teacher who sees a child struggling to keep up will ask, "Why am I not getting through to this kid?"

Perhaps most important, today's educators believe in taking action as soon as they — or parents — suspect a student has a learning disorder. That kind of early intervention helps a child's self-image. "If these kids are left alone, they begin to doubt themselves, and teachers begin to figure that child can't learn," Horowitz says. Discouraged and disheartened, these kids often lose their drive and enthusiasm for learning.

And kids who don't master skills such as reading run the risk of never catching up. So if you think your child has a learning disability, don't wait to seek help.

**What to do**

Get involved with your child's school. Observe the class, offer to help out, and develop a collaborative relationship with the school. Make sure the faculty knows you're supportive.

Next, talk to your child's teacher. Describe your concerns and ask how your child's progress compares to grade standards.

Then, arrange for testing through your child's school district. A team of educators can translate the test results and create an individualized education program (IEP) for your child. Under the U.S. Department of Education Individuals with Disabilities Education Act, kids with an identified learning disability are entitled to special instruction and accommodations.

Parents can also opt to consult private psychologists to glean more information on their child's cognitive skills and abilities.

Finally, be patient with and supportive of your child. Make learning fun by keeping frustration to a minimum and taking frequent breaks from homework.

Make sure your child knows he excels at something, says Horowitz. "It can be about how well they draw or how well they tell stories. Find things they can celebrate about themselves."

## CREATING THE RIGHT ENVIRONMENT FOR HOMEWORK

"Let's start the school year right," you tell your tween one September afternoon. "It's time to buckle down and establish good study habits. For starters, lose the iPod and the remote control. And while you're at it, color-coordinate your notebooks, keep an assignment checklist, and label your folders."

At least that's what you'd like to say. What you're probably saying — make that shouting — is more like this: "You've been texting for two hours now! Get off that cell phone and do your homework!"

Which brings us to the classic question about homework: Whose responsibility is it, anyway?

Certainly not the parents', educators will be quick to tell you. But they'll add a critical caveat to that: Parents must provide a home environment that's conducive to learning.

"The kind of environment kids need differs at every grade level," says Marilyn Price-Mitchell, cofounder of the National ParentNet Association, an organization that helps schools and parents increase parent involvement at school and home. "But making sure children have strategies to help them learn at home is what's most important for kids' success."

What strategies? It depends on the student. Each child is different, and parents need to find out just what works for theirs.

### Get organized

Here's something that works for just about every child: getting organized. For some kids, that means finding a way to help them remember what the assignments are. "We tell them, 'Get a three-ring binder and write everything down,'" says Eric Cohen, owner

## TIPS CREATING A HOMEWORK-FRIENDLY ENVIRONMENT

- Make sure the television isn't on — not even as background noise.
- Take your child to the library or the bookstore on a regular basis.
- Assume that your child will need to study every night.
- Ask your child if he understands his homework. If he doesn't, work a few examples together.
- Ask your child to show you his homework after the teacher returns it, to learn where he's having trouble and where he's doing well. See if your child did the work correctly.
- Stay in touch with your child's teacher. Ask about your child's class and what he is studying. Ask his teacher how you can support what he's studying (flash cards, spelling, etc.).
- Remember that you and the teacher want the same thing: to help your child learn.
- Don't be afraid to get in touch with the teacher if you and your child don't understand an assignment, or if your child is having a great deal of trouble. Almost all parents run into these problems, and teachers are generally glad to help.
- Don't do your child's work for him. Help him learn how to do it himself.
- Show your child that you think homework is important. If you are at work during homework time, ask to see his work when you get home.
- Praise your child for doing well. Make praise a habit.
- Ask your school about tips or guides for helping your child develop good study habits.
- Help an older student organize his assignments by recording them on calendars or planners, along with due dates, dates turned in, etc.

Source: The National Education Association

of Mercer Education, a Seattle-area tutoring and test-prep company. Parents should check those assignments — and make sure their child doesn't wait until the last minute to do them, he says.

Next, find your child a good workspace. "Where your child does his homework comes up a lot in parent discussions," Price-Mitchell says. "Should there be a computer in your child's room? Can you eliminate every distraction? These are things that are debated constantly."

A quiet environment is crucial. That means no interruptions — and no TV. "Kids need regularity and predictability," says Cohen. "They should know this is homework time. It's harder for kids to understand something is expected of them when there's chaos."

Become a partner with your child's teachers. What are the school's expectations? What are the other kids in the class doing? Be vigilant and responsive — but don't pester teachers or make unreasonable demands on them. "Parents must understand that teachers are often overwhelmed," Cohen says.

Connect with the other parents and compare notes. What kinds of time-management strategies do other families use in their homes? How do they set goals so that the big pieces of homework get done?

Don't do your child's homework for him; that won't help him learn. Sometimes, when a child hasn't done his homework, parents panic and step in. "The lesson the child learns is 'When I'm failing, my parents will bail me out,'" says Price-Mitchell.

Very young children may need guidance with assignments, but encourage your child to do as much as possible without your help. "If hand-holding goes on forever, kids won't develop independence or the confidence to develop skills on their own," Cohen says.

CHAPTER 8

# Math, Science, and More

■ ■ ■ ■ ■

## MAKING MATH MATTER

As parents, we value few skills more dearly than literacy. After all, reading opens the door to brand-new worlds, innovative ideas, and critical thinking. Literacy holds the key to learning.

Who doesn't revel in their child's first recitation of the ABCs? What proud parents don't crow — even a little bit — if their son or daughter turns out to be an early reader?

Funny, we never hear much about early adders. Or early subtractors, or even that occasional hyperprecocious kid who seems to intuitively recognize the relationship between integers. In fact, many of us, no math geniuses ourselves, laugh off our children's computation struggles with a "Guess she's just like me!" comment that translates into "It's OK if you don't do well in math."

It turns out it's not OK. A study published in 2008 by the U.S. Department of Education, "The Final Report of the National Mathematics Advisory Panel," concludes that as a nation, our math skills are declining. "There are consequences to a weakening of American independence and leadership in mathematics, the natural sciences, and engineering," the study reports. "We risk our ability to adapt to change. We risk technological surprise to our economic viability — and to the foundations of our country's security. National policy must ensure the healthy development of a domestic technical workforce of adequate scale with top-level skills."

The picture's even gloomier from a global perspective. Compared to math students around the world, our kids pretty much pale. Here's what the 2009 National Report Card indicates (the data was collected by the National Assessment of Educational Progress): Thirty-four percent of students in the United States score at or above proficiency level in eighth-grade math and thirty-nine percent score at proficiency level in fourth-grade math. According to the National Mathematics Advisory Panel, just 23 percent — not even one out of four! — of U.S. students show math competency at grade 12.

What does all this, well, add up to? Seems that in this country, we don't treat mathematics with enough respect, and our children feel the fallout. "Everyone is comfortable with reading," says Becca Lewis, a former elementary-school teacher. "Parents have this expectation that all kids learn to read. But math is less visible. It's harder to put in kids' hands; you don't have it sitting around your house, like books."

## MATH COUNTS

The reality is that math matters. "It can be a gatekeeper for a lot of kids," says Lewis, who is now a curriculum designer at DreamBox Learning, a Web-based math-learning tool. "If kids don't take enough math or score well on tests, countless education and career opportunities will be unavailable to them."

If your kids seem blasé about the education and job ops they risk missing, maybe they'll respond to real-life requirements: Mundane tasks such as shopping, dining out, and figuring out mileage and budgets for trips all take numbers know-how.

"You don't need to be math literate only if you want to become an astronaut," says Sarah Daniels, a former Stanford math major who's now marketing vice president for DreamBox. "You can't buy a house, balance your checkbook, or decide whether it's better to buy a product at Costco or the grocery store without math. But in our math-starved society, we've forgotten that."

Teachers try their best to get students up to speed in math. But many teachers these days are undertrained and underfunded. "Teachers frequently lack things they need, like paper or ink, or hands-on materials kids can use to model their thinking," says Lewis. And teacher-prep programs often go light on the math content. Lewis, who learned to teach kindergarten through eighth-grade math in a program that offered a semester-long weekly math/science course, supplemented her own training with additional instruction.

It doesn't help that no one seems to agree on teaching methods. This, of course, is nothing new. Ever since "arithmetic" became "math" with the introduction of New Math in the Space Race '60s,

## TIPS MAKING MATH MATTER

- Play number games during everyday activities, such as counting the number of steps, the number of items going into the laundry, or the number of trucks you see while driving.
- Read the calendar and determine the number of days until an upcoming event. With older children, count by sevens.
- Plan a shopping list and figure out how to shop for items that fit your budget.
- With your young child, count the number of items you bought at the store.
- Read a recipe and have your child measure the amounts for the ingredients.
- Have your child practice counting the change needed to pay for an item.
- At the grocery store, ask your child to find items that are triangles, circles, rectangles, and other shapes.
- Ask your child to recognize or stack the groceries you bought by container shape.
- Take measurements for a project around the house.
- Compare and organize tools, dishes, or other objects based on size, color, or weight.
- Find ways to collect and organize information.
- Have your child help sort the laundry by various categories — by color or size, for example.
- As you're shopping, compare the amounts listed in the "Nutrition Facts" on packaged foods.
- Read charts with your child, such as weather charts or movie schedules.
- Play card games that require counting and keeping score, such as dominos, checkers, Chinese checkers, or Chutes and Ladders.

Source: DreamBox Learning, *dreambox.com*

coaching kids to multiply, divide, and compute algebraic equations has generated controversy. For example: Is your child's math program based on inquiry or does it focus on the basics? Ask around; the impassioned thinking and divergent views on this topic may surprise you.

"There has been a dumbing-down of content, standards, and expectations in schools," says Bob Brandt, a founding member of Where's The Math?, an advocacy group that works to restore rigor to math education.

Where's The Math? organizers call current math trends "fuzzy" and support a program that emphasizes fundamental computational skills. "If parents are technically trained, they look at their child's math curriculum and think, 'How will my child have the potential to do the kind of work I'm doing?'" says Brandt.

**Bringing math home**

While the math-ed hotshots battle it out, where does that leave parents and kids? With any luck, at home, engaging in number-rich games and activities.

No one is asking you to solve logic problems (second-graders can do them, but they make grownups dizzy) or do a fact triangle (don't ask). Simply make counting, patterns, and numbers part of your child's routine.

Driving someplace? Notice which exit number is coming up — and show your child how they appear sequentially. If your child is a toddler, sing counting songs along the way, such as "One, Two, Buckle My Shoe."

Read counting books to your youngster, such as *Counting Crocodiles* by Judy Sierra and Will Hillenbrand, *Counting on Frank* by Rod Clement, or *My Little Counting Book* by Roger Priddy. Then create your own counting book with your preschooler or kindergartener. Ask your child to draw four balls to illustrate the number four, and so on.

As kids get older, play board games with them that require math skills and score keeping, such as Yahtzee, checkers, and Chutes and Ladders.

"Add math to your child's daily life in small ways, like a vitamin," says Lewis. "That will help them think about math more positively."

## KEEPING GIRLS INTERESTED IN SCIENCE

Not long after Mary Margaret Callahan took a physics exam at Whitman College in Walla Walla, Washington, in the late '90s, her professor said to the class: "Gentlemen, I am so embarrassed. Every girl scored higher than every boy in this class. But don't worry, men, trend is not destiny."

A few short years after that, Lawrence Summers, then president of Harvard University, told an academic conference that innate differences between men and women could be one reason fewer women succeed in math and science careers.

Ultimately, Summers (now head of the National Economic Council) resigned from his position, Callahan became a science and math specialist at the Seattle Girls School, and the rest of us were left to wonder once again just how far females really have come on the educational playing field.

Apparently, not far enough. "In certain science careers, such as computer engineering, women are sorely underrepresented," says Stacey Roberts-Ohr, executive director of Expanding Your Horizons Network, a California-based organization that encourages young women to pursue careers in the fields of science, math, and engineering. "We are trying to fix that."

An advocacy group called the Math/Science Network says female membership in the National Academy of Sciences is just 10 percent — and the number of women earning doctorates in mathematics is declining. In addition, the National Center for Women and Information Technology found that while girls took 56 percent of all advanced placement (AP) tests in 2006, they made up just 15 percent of students taking the AP computer science test.

The math/science world hasn't looked this dismal for girls since the first talking Barbie doll exclaimed, "Math class is tough!"

It's not that young girls shun math and science. They do just fine — in fact, they often excel — until they hit middle school, according to Rafael del Castillo, a former science and math teacher who is now assistant head of the Seattle Girls School. "They lose confidence before they lose competence," he says.

The reason? Girls tend to gather information collaboratively, he says. "They want to explore the process more and go a little deeper

— to know the why and the how. Boys are more focused on the answer. They want to do it quickly and get it right."

Teachers respond with enthusiasm to the male find-the-answer-fast learning model in math and science classes, del Castillo says. That turns the boys into the "good" students — the ones the teacher rewards — while the girls learn to see themselves as minor players. And that's how self-confidence begins to ebb.

Without constructive experiences, girls won't stay in science, says Nancy Ruzycki, Ph.D., a former University of Washington research scientist who teaches math and physics at Seattle's Chief Sealth High School. Not that all Ruzycki's own experiences have been constructive. Back in high school chemistry, she remembers, the teacher would shout "Beauty school!" if a female student spoke out of turn.

#### Finding role models

It doesn't escape these educators and scientists that strong role models — women who have blazed trails in the math, science, and tech worlds — have never achieved the visibility of, say, Hannah Montana. "There must be good images out there of creative, successful women," says Callahan. "But what do girls see on TV? America's top model? They need mentors."

Chances are they won't find them in elementary school. Grade-school teachers, usually generalists, are not highly trained in science, Ruzycki says. And most high school math and science departments are overwhelmingly male.

That leaves middle school, during which the social scene claims center stage. "Girls think, 'Do I want boys to like me, or do I want to be the smart girl? Can I be a good student and be pretty and popular?'" says Callahan. "At that age, it's hard for them to see themselves as a little of everything."

They're clearly not seeing themselves as computer scientists.

"The perception is that computer science is either a male field or a field for geeks," says Mylene Padolina, senior diversity consultant for DigiGirlz High Technology Camps. Since 2000, Microsoft has sponsored DigiGirlz Camps, a summer camp for girls that introduces them to careers in the technology industry. The free camps are held throughout the country.

## TIPS KEEPING GIRLS INTERESTED IN SCIENCE AND MATH

- Provide role models and mentors for your daughter in the math, science, and tech worlds.
- Expose your daughter to the myriad jobs in these fields.
- Make sure you know what is going on in your daughter's science and math classrooms. Are teachers responding more to boys who go for the quick answers?
- If your daughter is beginning to lose interest in math or science, talk to the instructor and try to find out why.
- Look into summer science or technology camps for your daughter.
- Consider sending her to an all-girls school.

Technology, as Padolina points out, is not just a guy thing. "We want girls to understand there are lots of kinds of jobs in tech fields," she says. "At Microsoft, there are programmers, developers, and testers – but also psychologists, graphic artists, and people in other disciplines."

It's a curious paradox that young women – more of them than ever – are training to become physicians. According to the Association of American Medical Colleges, the number of women applying to medical schools in the United States increases yearly; women now make up about 50 percent of all applicants.

Why do females sign up for bio class, but take a pass on engineering and physics? Less than 20 percent of doctorates in physics go to women, notes Ruzycki, who has one.

Everyone has a theory. Ruzycki feels it's because medicine is generating a plethora of female role models. "Young women run into other women in biological and medical fields, and that makes a big difference," she says. "Women in medicine can mentor other women and develop a work/life balance."

Roberts-Ohr says women gravitate toward careers that help others. "In medicine, they feel they're making a contribution," she says. "They don't see how computer science relates to the greater good. They think they'd be stuck behind a desk, programming all day."

But before — way before — your daughter decides on a career in medicine or engineering or a stint at Microsoft, she needs to stay engaged in the math and science world. How can you help that happen?

Del Castillo is a big proponent of all-girls schools. "Parents need to look at their child and decide which kind of environment works best," he says. "A single-sex option should be considered. If girls lose confidence or interest early, they will start down a different path."

## WHAT THAT REPORT CARD REALLY MEANS

"Tries hard to pay attention." "Enjoys socializing with other students." "Accepts redirection well."

Educators call this "teacherspeak." Here's the translation: Your child is not paying attention, talks too much in class, and won't stay on task.

Why the sugarcoating? Would you prefer a report that says your kid speaks out of turn and has attention issues?

Such jargon adds even more mystery and confusion to the report card muddle, already a common source of anxiety among parents and students. Many parents view report cards as much more than the measure of their child's learning, progress, and growth. Somehow these descriptions and grades have evolved into the holy grail of education — a way to quantify achievement and reward success.

All that angst often comes from our own inner child, says tutoring company director Susan Small. Parents unwittingly reenact report card experiences gleaned from their own early memories. "They'll think, 'My parents became really mad if I got less than a B,'" she says. "They're surprised when they realize they are following that same path."

And even if that inner child is silent, the outer culture is deafening. Who can minimize report cards when your child is facing a world that's raised the bar on standardized testing, advanced-placement classes, and designer colleges? "Parents are thinking, 'My kid better be getting a 4.0 and taking APs [advanced placement tests] just to have a shot,'" Small says.

While written comments remain the conventional way to measure an elementary school student's progress, kids — and their parents — often encounter letter grades for the first time in middle school.

It can be a shock.

Some parents see these first grades as "the writing on the wall" — an irrevocable indication of things to come.

But that's not so, contends Wendy Lawrence, a Seattle-area teacher and former middle school head. "A child adjusting to middle school can go through many different phases," she says. "Some kids come in and they just get it. Some don't have their organizational skills in place yet; it might take them the full year. And other kids fall somewhere in between."

While grades can show trends — a math grade, for example, might evolve from a C one semester into an A the next — they don't mean much by themselves. "They can't tell you what you need to change, how to study better, or how to do your homework," says Lawrence.

Grades also reflect the standards that a particular school, class, or teacher has set. Those standards may vary considerably — even within the same school. Students should know what counts. Does one teacher value class participation and another appreciate punctuality? Do preparation and effort matter? If expectations seem vague, kids should speak up and find out what they are. No one likes to be caught by surprise.

## TIPS RESPONDING TO A POOR REPORT CARD

- Find out what class expectations are.
- Don't overemphasize the importance of grades.
- Keep your child involved in other projects and activities.
- Talk with your child and his teacher if grades or teacher comments are poor.
- If your child needs extra assistance, help him get organized or hire a tutor for one-on-one coaching.
- Stay involved. Know what's going on in the classroom and how your child is doing.

### Facing a poor report card

It's one thing to intellectualize and try to understand the elements that go into school evaluations. It's another to face a report card that's disappointing — and a potential blot on your child's record.

Try not to overreact, teachers advise. Chances are, the child is already feeling bad. He may pretend not to care, but don't believe it; most children want to do well. Talk to your child and find out how he thinks he's been doing — and what he could have done better.

Next, speak with your child's teacher. "Approach it in an information-gathering way, such as, 'I'm investigating this grade. Can you give me your feedback?'" Small suggests. Find out if there are behavioral or organizational issues that you, your child, and the teacher can address.

Instructors, especially in high school, typically include a rubric (scoring guide) on written assignments and offer a course syllabus outlining expectations. Parents should figure out what those are and what each grade really means.

Then, find ways to help. That might mean working with your child on organizational or time-management skills, or even hiring a tutor for some one-on-one coaching. Don't be afraid to offer your youngster incentives or rewards.

If things don't improve, have your child assessed for potential learning problems. The assessment should include a look at the child's emotional status.

Most important, don't overemphasize grades. Focus on essays, art projects, sports, or other endeavors. Don't let your child feel that grades are everything.

## WHEN YOUR CHILD IS GIFTED

We've all met a few of them: The three-year-old who orders off the menu. The four-year-old who can name all the states and their capitals. The two-year-old who can add and subtract; and the kindergartener whose vocabulary is so advanced you'd like to elect him senator.

We call them "gifted," though some educators prefer the label "highly capable."

Terminology aside, we're talking about very bright children who typically score 130 or higher on IQ tests — placing them in the top 2 percent to 3 percent of the population.

If your child is one of these kids, chances are you already know. "Parents can usually recognize if their child is advanced in some way — with vocabulary, for example, or with numbers," says Nancy Robinson, Ph.D., professor emerita at the University of Washington. "And parents are generally right about their children; they can trust their gut instincts."

Parents might notice their child is unusually good at jigsaw puzzles and has an excellent memory. Or they may discover their child is exceptionally creative.

Gifted children also possess excellent problem-solving abilities, long attention spans, remarkable curiosity, a great sense of humor, and the ability to learn quickly, according to the "Characteristics of Giftedness" scale developed by Linda Kreger Silverman, who directs the Gifted Development Center in Denver, Colorado.

Often, gifted children have different emotional needs than other youngsters. "They are much more sensitive and perfectionistic; there's an inflexibility about their thinking; it may be hard for them to see other points of view," says Wilder Dominick, head of the Open Window School in Bellevue, Washington.

According to the National Association for Gifted Children, gifted kids are often very curious — and very observant. They use adult-sounding words and reasoning, often coming up with unusual ideas. Gifted kids recognize complex patterns and come up with surprising solutions to problems. They often have excellent memories.

Should you have your child tested? Yes, if there's a reason for it, such as applying to a gifted school or program. Otherwise, experts advise, wait until it serves a purpose. In other words, don't test for the sake of testing.

In the meantime, immerse your child in activities, books, and interests that promote investigation and imagination, suggests Michael Murphy, head of Seattle Country Day School, a school for gifted children. "Instead of an easy puzzle, find hands-on pursuits in which kids can explore creating and designing their own projects," Murphy says. "These kinds of things allow for divergent thinking."

### Education options

Let's say you've concluded your child is gifted. Now what? For starters, relax. Parents often feel they must provide the perfect environment if they have a gifted child, but many — even most — will thrive in less-than-ideal classrooms, says psychologist Gail Rosenberg, Ph.D. "You have to be a good-enough parent, not a perfect parent." Still, some experts say there is value in finding an appropriately challenging program for gifted kids. "People often assume that a child who is gifted will succeed anywhere," Dominick says. "This is not true. Gifted children have a set of needs that are very difficult to meet — and are very complex."

Robinson agrees. "The bright kids won't do fine on their own; they'll rev down their motors and go along with the flow. Some will become discouraged and depressed."

Parents should seek an educational program that fuels their child's curiosity and encourages discovery and high-level thinking, Dominick advises. "Bright kids don't need as much time on drill and practice. They think outside the box and synthesize ideas. If things are too predictable, these kids will lose engagement."

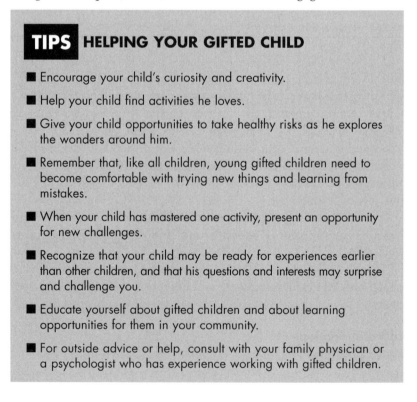

### TIPS HELPING YOUR GIFTED CHILD

- Encourage your child's curiosity and creativity.
- Help your child find activities he loves.
- Give your child opportunities to take healthy risks as he explores the wonders around him.
- Remember that, like all children, young gifted children need to become comfortable with trying new things and learning from mistakes.
- When your child has mastered one activity, present an opportunity for new challenges.
- Recognize that your child may be ready for experiences earlier than other children, and that his questions and interests may surprise and challenge you.
- Educate yourself about gifted children and about learning opportunities for them in your community.
- For outside advice or help, consult with your family physician or a psychologist who has experience working with gifted children.

Children need to be around other kids who "speak their language," share the depth of their interests, understand their jokes, and move at about the same speed, Robinson says. "Kids want to fit in, and when they feel too different from their classmates, as they often do in a regular classroom, they can be miserable."

That's why students who excel in a variety of subjects often benefit from a learning environment — whether it's a special school or classroom — that's self-contained and geared for similar learners. "This is one time that I advocate ignoring children's wishes, specifically their preference to stay put with the classmates they know," Robinson says. "Most kids will be loyal to their friends and scared to lose them. They don't have your confidence that they will, in fact, make new friends who are an even better match in interests than the ones they know."

Other options? Robinson suggests "cluster grouping" bright kids in regular classrooms. This involves grouping a handful of gifted students together so they can work cooperatively and feed off one another's ideas.

Highly gifted kids at the far end of the spectrum sometimes enter high school or college at an early age. The University of Washington's Early Entrance Program, for example, admits sixteen scholars younger than age fifteen into its Transition School. These teens (or younger) become full-time UW students the following year.

If a child has no access to a specially designed program, parents should request a private conference with their child's teacher, Robinson suggests. Ask the teacher to try something new and innovative. Could this first-grade child do math with the second-graders? Could he be excused from reading so he could work on another project?

Parents, Robinson says, must act as their child's advocates. "Teachers are overwhelmed. Even though they have your child's interest at heart, your child could fall through the cracks," she says.

Often, parents regret not enrolling their gifted child in a special class when the child was younger. Sometimes a child — by now turned off and disinterested in learning — no longer qualifies for the advanced class, and sometimes the class is simply full, Robinson says. "If you don't apply for special opportunities that are available early on, later access may be limited."

## Q & A WITH NANCY ROBINSON, PH.D.

*Dr. Robinson is professor emerita of psychiatry and behavioral sciences at the University of Washington and former director of the UW Halbert and Nancy Robinson Center for Young Scholars.*

**Q: In what ways do gifted children differ from other kids?**

Gifted youngsters come from all sorts of backgrounds and probably have about the same range of characteristics as any other group with one exception: In some ways, their development is significantly advanced. It's totally arbitrary how high a line we draw before we decide that a child is sufficiently advanced to be called "highly capable." The most important criterion is whether their talents are such that they need something more than the usual range of experiences provided for their age group.

**Q: What do we mean by "academically gifted"?**

When we think of gifted children in school, it's children advanced in academics (and, in high school, athletics) whom we identify, but children can be gifted in the creative and performing arts, in chess, in leadership, and so on. Academically advanced children are also more advanced in mental maturity — and often in personal-social maturity — than are other children of the same age. On average (and there is a wide range of differences here), academically gifted children are more personally mature than their chronological age, but not quite as personally mature as their mental age, and some don't seem mature at all, or they seem mature only at some times and not others.

**Q: Do gifted children have emotional traits that can distinguish them from other kids?**

The jury is still out about this question, although gifted children can certainly seem more sensitive and intense than other children at times. They understand so much more of what they're exposed to, such as the implications of a disturbing concept (such as infinity or death), a mildly critical comment from a teacher, or something disturbing they see on TV, but don't have the emotional calluses that come with experience. Their fears are like those of older children. It's harder for them to shrug something off or put it aside.

**Q: Are there different levels of giftedness?**

It's possible, within even a special classroom, to find as wide a range of difference in, say, IQ, as between those who are mildly gifted and those with mild intellectual disabilities. Let's take a third-grade class of gifted eight-year-olds. To get in, children are probably a couple of years advanced. But a few will be four years advanced, and a few even more.

As you go up the scale, the children become rarer and rarer. To use IQ as a marker, about 5 percent of children have IQs of 125 or higher, about 2 percent have IQs of 130 or higher, but only about one-tenth of 1 percent have IQs of 145 or higher.

**Q: What are the downsides of failing to address a gifted child's educational needs?**

Every child deserves to love school, to get up every morning with something to look forward to. When children have already mastered what they are being "taught," when they are ready for so much more, the light goes out of their eyes and the school day seems endless. They disengage. Even the best-hearted child is likely to become irritated with classmates who seem to take forever on what is "obvious," when the day goes like a slow-motion movie. When an appropriate challenge comes along, they are likely to avoid it, because they are so used to gliding along with little effort. Their work habits and intellectual courage suffer. Worst of all, their image of their own competence suffers as soon as they come up against anything difficult; they have become fragile and lack resilience.

**Q: What can families do if their school district doesn't offer programs for highly capable children?**

If there is nothing in place that seems a likely fit for your child, there are still some things a parent can do:

- Seek psychological testing of your child's reasoning ability and academic achievement to back up your own observations.
- Share with your child's teacher what you are seeing at home that lets you know that your child's engagement is lagging, and brainstorm some classroom activities that would be more challenging.
- Inquire whether your child might spend part, or even all, of the day with older students.

- Explore online courses that might be substituted in areas your child has already mastered. (You may need to pay for these courses yourself.)
- Enroll your child in special classes in the summer, to expose her to other children of similar interests and maturity.
- Consider an independent school (though not all independent schools will be a better fit than public schools). Home schooling for all or part of the day is also an option.
- Plead with the principal to try the "cluster grouping" of bright students next year.

**Q: What else can parents do?**

Parenting a gifted child is labor intensive. Sometimes, if your child feels out of place, you'll need to be a temporary best friend. Your child will also "use up" activities at a great rate — borrow more books from the library, do more science experiments at home, want to go more places and learn more — than other children. And you may be looking for out-of-the-ordinary chances for your child to meet other people with similar interests but differing ages — a chess club, photography club, drawing or ceramics class, youth symphony — so that they can find company at their own mental age level, develop their special talents, and deepen their sense of who they are.

For talent to develop, people have to work hard, persist in the face of challenge, and have the desire. You'll help this along by not praising your child for how smart or talented they are, but rather, praising their efforts, their thoughtfulness, what they've learned from their mistakes, and how much they've grown in the process.

## HOW TO NURTURE YOUR CHILD'S TALENT

My mother thought I was a piano prodigy because I could play Chopin's "Minute Waltz" in fifty seconds.

My childhood unfolded accordingly: plenty of practicing, recitals, and music competitions. Our house teemed with passionate dedication to the craft. The dedication was my mother's, not mine, and by age sixteen, I began to engage in less lofty teenage pursuits. Soon after that, I took up guitar, for which I had absolutely no talent.

The good news: I did find my passion — writing — and worked tenaciously to develop that skill. The great news: I can still play the "Minute Waltz" — at an impressively slow speed.

There's no shocking moral to this familiar vignette. Everyone knows that whether we're talking music, dance, art, or athletics, talent plus commitment plus encouragement can foster success. Trouble is, you typically need all three. Talent — even plenty of it — is never enough.

And true talent — the Yo-Yo Ma kind of talent (not only did he play the cello for Barack Obama's inauguration, at age seven he played for President Kennedy) — surfaces quite rarely. That's why Michael Jordan is, well, Michael Jordan, and that's why, try as they might, movie-studio execs will never find another Shirley Temple.

"You'd be surprised how many parents think their child is a gifted musical genius," says Diane Williams, who, as piano director at the Suzuki Institute of Seattle, should know. "It's usually not the case."

### What it takes

While Williams rarely sees extraordinary talent, she does see extraordinary students. That's because they work at it. "What it takes is extremely keen interest and commitment," she says. "I've had students who I thought would never get it. I've thought of telling them, 'Try soccer.' And then they end up being incredibly amazing."

Cindy Frank-Linkon runs The Studio, a fine-arts program in Bellevue, Washington. Frank-Linkon often spots talented students, but knows kids "can only get so far with that." She believes in teaching students the basics and watching where that takes them. "Every child has some ability. They might not even know they have it," she says. "They can all learn to draw and paint — and they all get better as they go along."

But how about that rare tot who throws a mean curve ball or taps out "Ode to Joy" on her Fisher-Price baby grand? Don't her parents have an obligation to help nurture and develop her skills?

Absolutely, say experts. Just don't rush to enlist the private coaches or invest in the Steinway. Remember that raw ability, coupled with interest and perseverance, can emerge later — and in a completely different field.

That's why parents should introduce their youngsters to an assortment of options and activities. "Your job is to expose them to lots of different things and then observe what they choose to spend their time on," says Paula Olszewski-Kubilius, author of *Early Gifts: Recognizing and Nurturing Children's Talents.* "Make sure you stay open-minded. Kids do change."

And that's why you should rethink those grandiose plans you've got for your four-year-old tennis phenom. Yes, there's always that very, very slim chance he's headed for Wimbledon. More likely, he's a precocious athlete who you'd like to see achieve the superstar status you've always craved.

"So much of the early talent thing is projection," says psychologist Mogel. "Many parents measure their own worth and effectiveness by their child's success." And, Mogel says, it's not unusual for kids to show fleeting "bursts of precocity" that soon fade.

### Zeroing in

Elisa Barston wants to make sure her daughter, Melia, develops a broad range of interests. That's why Melia, six and a half, takes gym, ballet, and Chinese classes. "I want her to find things she loves," says Barston.

Melia also studies violin, and has been doing that since she was three and a half. It's that instrument which clearly claims top spot in the Barston family. Elisa Barston is the Seattle Symphony principal second violin and former associate concertmaster of the St. Louis Symphony Orchestra. Her own mother, a cellist, studied at Juilliard, and her husband, an orthopedic surgeon, also plays the violin. Clearly, Melia is growing up in a house infused with a culture that covets music.

Odds are, Melia's got talent and lots of it. Yet Barston downplays talent and spotlights traits such as persistence, determination, and commitment. She internalized those values growing up and hopes Melia will absorb them, as well.

In Melia's world, music is a given — just like school, homework, and family dinners. "You practice every day that you eat, sleep, and study," Barston says. "It's your job." Melia doesn't always embrace her job with joy. "She'll say, 'I don't want to practice.' I tell her this is one of the things we do," says Barston.

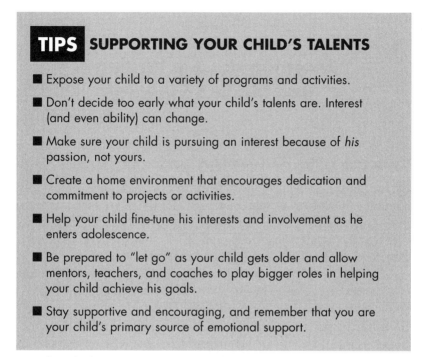

## TIPS SUPPORTING YOUR CHILD'S TALENTS

- Expose your child to a variety of programs and activities.
- Don't decide too early what your child's talents are. Interest (and even ability) can change.
- Make sure your child is pursuing an interest because of *his* passion, not yours.
- Create a home environment that encourages dedication and commitment to projects or activities.
- Help your child fine-tune his interests and involvement as he enters adolescence.
- Be prepared to "let go" as your child gets older and allow mentors, teachers, and coaches to play bigger roles in helping your child achieve his goals.
- Stay supportive and encouraging, and remember that you are your child's primary source of emotional support.

Often, kids opt out when the going gets tough. "They are not old or mature enough to understand the value of music; that it's a blessing to learn it," she says. "It breaks my heart when parents just let their children quit."

While exposing kids to a variety of classes makes sense when they're young, it makes less sense once they find a focus, experts say. So when should kids start shedding their multitude of activities and — if they find a passion — zero in on just one? Olszewski-Kubilius says by middle school, they should make some choices. "That's when you want to see them pursuing their field of interest."

And that's when you want to give your kids some space. For parents, this means backing off and letting teachers and coaches start to play bigger roles in your children's lives.

Still, parents must stay engaged. "Kids go through ups and downs in interest, and sometimes they need a break," Olszewski-Kubilius says. "Parents are the child's first teacher — and the child's most important emotional support."

CHAPTER 9

# Learning to Love Writing and Public Speaking

## KEEP THE LOVE OF WRITING (NOT TEXTING!) ALIVE

Have you glanced at a tween's text messages lately? No? How about her email or instant messages (IMs)? If you take a peek, you'll find plenty of sentence fragments, emoticons, and shortcuts like LOL (laugh out loud) and BFF (best friends forever). Punctuation? Forget about it.

Which begs the question: Where has all the good writing gone?

Chances are, you won't find it anywhere near the world of electronic communication. Even blogging tends to be informal, as do the observations and insights teens share on their Facebook pages.

Is this a bad omen for the good old reliable research paper and the quintessential five-paragraph essay?

Could be, according to a recent study by the Pew Internet & American Life Project, a think tank that produces reports on the impact of the Internet.

While teens don't think technology has an impact on their writing, many of the kids surveyed said the e-writing style does filter into their schoolwork. "Overall, nearly two-thirds of teens say they incorporate some informal styles from their text-based communications into their writing at school," the study states.

As if that's not enough to induce panic in the hearts of literacy devotees, here's more: Only about a third of the country's eighth-graders are proficient writers, according to the U.S. Department of Education study "The Nation's Report Card: Writing 2007." The findings did note some improvements: The average writing score for eighth-graders in 2007 was three points higher than in 2002 and six points higher than in 1998.

There's a growing awareness among educators that kids need writing skills for life, not just to pass high school English or a state-mandated standardized test. Writing — all forms of it — matters, no matter what field kids pursue, says Julie Manley, a Seattle-area language arts teacher. "A scientist needs to publish well-written papers. An employer expects employees to be able to write." And yes, it's even important, she says, to be able to transmit readable, coherent email.

### What schools teach

Schools begin teaching writing fundamentals — including sentence structure, mechanics, and paragraphing — in the elementary school years. By middle school, writing expectations rise, and so do the depth and details of reading and writing assignments. That's when students begin to find their own voice in their writing, and learn to incorporate more sophisticated literary techniques into their work.

By sixth grade or so, a student might be asked to progress from standard book-report regurgitation to thoughtful essays produced in narrative or expository style. Writing may become more inventive, with students injecting dialogue, description, or in-depth analysis into their papers. Essays begin to reflect a higher level of critical thinking.

Patti Crouch, a high school English teacher, teaches her ninth-graders ways to set up an argument. By the time the students hit their senior year, they're ready to grapple with more complex ideas.

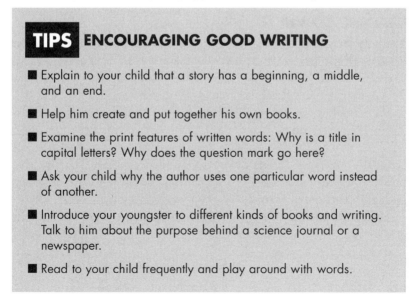

#### TIPS ENCOURAGING GOOD WRITING

- Explain to your child that a story has a beginning, a middle, and an end.
- Help him create and put together his own books.
- Examine the print features of written words: Why is a title in capital letters? Why does the question mark go here?
- Ask your child why the author uses one particular word instead of another.
- Introduce your youngster to different kinds of books and writing. Talk to him about the purpose behind a science journal or a newspaper.
- Read to your child frequently and play around with words.

Still, today's English and literature instructors don't stop at imbuing their students with reasoning and critical-thinking skills. The five-paragraph essay is alive and well and thriving in middle and high schools.

Why has this venerable essay form endured for so many years? "It's a structure to hang ideas on," says Crouch. "It's rudimentary, like learning scales." This form — which includes an introduction, supporting body, evidence, and conclusion — works for everything from science reports to personal letters and term papers, and helps students get their ideas across clearly, she notes.

While educators make certain they expose students to creative writing, language arts teachers — especially in middle and high school — focus more on structured and analytical writing than on the genres of fiction, poetry, and narratives we commonly think of as "creative." The reason? College comes next — and along with it, endless research-driven reports and the ubiquitous written final exam.

Students who learn to find their own voice and style in their writing have a sense that their own ideas count, says Crouch. "They are the kids who read a lot, and who talk about books and politics with their parents."

## READING TO WRITE

You've gotten the memo: Read to your baby. Read to your toddler. Read to your six-year-old, even if he can read to himself. Read rhyming books, fairy tales, short stories, long ones — heck, read *People* magazine, if that's what keeps you reading.

Here's what we know: Reading to your child helps him learn about language, objects, people, and places. It nurtures the bond between you and your youngster, and sends the message that books are really awesome things to have around. Eventually, kids realize books open up entire new worlds and experiences for those lucky enough to become engrossed in their pages.

Here's what you might not know: Reading fosters writing. In fact — and I'll go out on a limb here — you can't be a writer unless you're a reader.

Now, not everyone who picks up a Harry Potter book intends to pen the next best-selling fantasy novel. And few of us recite

*Cat in a Hat* to our little ones hoping they'll one day one-up Thing One.

But think about it. Can you compose music without hearing the masters perform it? Can you paint without feasting your eyes on glorious works of art?

We need models because we learn from them, digest them, and integrate their vision and creativity into the recesses of our minds. Good music, art, and writing are infectious. The more we're around those sounds and images, the more they seep into our pores and elevate our tastes until we come up with new definitions of what we consider "good."

As a child, I'd fashion little sheets out of cardboard, scribble a few sentences on each page, and add a doodle here and there. I'd patch the collection together to create a primitive yet highly original "book," although I'm certain I borrowed heavily from some early reader and poached a line or two from *Dick and Jane.*

These days, when I crave inspiration or face a writing task and come up utterly empty, I turn to Dave Eggers or Anne Tyler or Anna Quindlen, and they invariably get me back on track. My poaching days, however, are over.

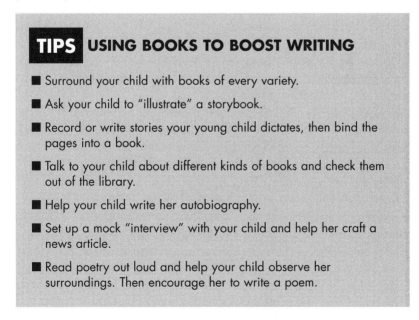

## TIPS USING BOOKS TO BOOST WRITING

- Surround your child with books of every variety.
- Ask your child to "illustrate" a storybook.
- Record or write stories your young child dictates, then bind the pages into a book.
- Talk to your child about different kinds of books and check them out of the library.
- Help your child write her autobiography.
- Set up a mock "interview" with your child and help her craft a news article.
- Read poetry out loud and help your child observe her surroundings. Then encourage her to write a poem.

Can you awaken the writer in your young reader or even younger future reader? Yes, you can, with a little thought and some out-of-the-book thinking.

Once kids can draw, they can begin "writing." Read them a picture book — say, *Goodnight Moon* — and ask them to think about the toy house, toy mouse, or other knickknacks they spot in their own room. Using crayons, pencils, or paint, they can illustrate those objects. The picture need not be a masterpiece; the idea is to tell a story that reflects the one they've been told.

As they get a bit older, help them use their drawings to build a sequential story. This might include story elements such as a beginning, some kind of plot or action, a "what happens next" component, and an ending.

The next step? Have them describe what happens on each page while you record their thoughts and words below their art. Bind the pages together — use tape, staples, or ring binders — and present them with their first personally created work of fiction.

### Explore different genres

Grade school kids benefit from family discussions about books, writers, and writing genres. Maybe they've read a book about Helen Keller. That would be a good time to talk to them about biographies. Visit the library and check out some biographies and autobiographies for children, then ask them what they'd like to include in their own autobiography.

Feeling ambitious? Write your own brief autobiography, then help your kids begin theirs. Sample chapters: My Favorite Vacations; Why I Liked (or Didn't Like) First Grade; Birthday Parties and Other Celebrations; Friends, Relatives, and Other Special People.

Show them a newspaper (yes, a real paper, not a virtual one) and describe the life and times of a news reporter. Then set up a mock interview. Help your child come up with questions, morph into Cinderella or Spiderman or Gabriella from *High School Musical* and then — here's the fun part — invent the answers (don't feel guilty; real-life people in high places do that all the time!). Then help your child craft a simple "article" about his or her celebrity subject, using a real, published profile as a model.

Kids go wild for poetry, especially the rhythmic, rhyming kind. From an early age, they warm to the verses of Sandra Boynton, Dr. Seuss, and Shel Silverstein. Older children enjoy collections by Jack Prelutsky, a writer who knows how to make poetry fun. His animated, witty books include *It's Raining Pigs & Noodles* and *Behold the Bold Umbrellaphant.*

Read the rhymes out loud, and don't be afraid to experiment with a variety of sounds and styles. Talk to your kids about where writers find ideas for their poems. Then take a walk together and jot down cool things you see. Or plant yourselves at a coffee shop or a park and look around. Maybe you'll see a girl wearing a crazy hat or a puppy sipping a double-tall cappuccino.

Poetry can be serious or silly; it can revel in grand, important things or in nothing at all. Encourage your child to pick a topic or two and play with words and phrases, using a favorite poet's style as a template.

Then go ahead and give it a try yourself. You just might enjoy it.

## Q & A WITH MEG LIPPERT

*Meg Lippert is a teacher, professor, storyteller, and award-winning author (or co-author) of 22 books of multicultural folktales, including* The Talking Vegetables.

**Q: How can parents get children interested in writing?**
Read aloud, and always read the name of the author and illustrator. Tell children that people wrote the books they love, and that they, too, can write their own stories. Make a wide variety of drawing and writing supplies easily available to children, and rave about what they write and draw. Write down stories they tell you and make simple booklets of their stories, letting them draw pictures and later on encouraging them to write a sentence or two on each page.

**Q: How can we foster creativity in our children's writing?**
Turn off the TV and be actively involved in your child's play. Stories emerge out of a child's interaction with his or her world, whether it's a trip to the grocery store or a walk around the block. You can encourage children to think creatively by asking "What if . . ." questions; then be a good listener. Remember to

share stories from your culture and from cultures different from yours. Multicultural folktales broaden a child's experience and expose your child to the creative imaginations of a wide variety of people from different heritages.

**Q: What is "storytelling" and how does it help kids become readers and writers?**

"Storytelling" is sharing stories you know, or have learned, with a listener or listeners. And you can tell stories anywhere — in the car, waiting in line, while chopping vegetables, around the dinner table, snuggled next to your child in bed.

The stories many children most love to hear are stories of you and stories of themselves. Tell children simple folktales you know, such as "The Three Bears" or "The Three Billy Goats Gruff." Children love to hear the same familiar stories over and over, and soon your child will be telling these with you, chiming in on repeated phrases, like "Who's been eating my porridge?" and repeated sound words, like "trip, trap, trip, trap." You and your child can even write your own versions of these stories. And stories that you make up, especially if they feature your child as the hero/heroine, inspire children to write them down.

**Q: Are there activities outside of school that can help develop and foster writers?**

Everything your child does is raw material for storytelling and story writing. The more varied the activities you do with your child, and the more you talk about them together, the more language fluency and story ideas your child will gather.

Make yourself and your child at home in your local library and your local bookstore. Take your child to story hours. Make his or her next birthday party a "Meet the Author" party, where children are the authors and write storybooks together. Ask your child to help you pick out favorite books for friends' birthday gifts.

**Q: How can we help our children experience the joy of writing?**

Block out 15 minutes every week to write with your child. When you listen openly and enthusiastically to your child's stories of his or her day, and write one of the stories down in a weekly journal, you will build a treasury of memories that will be your child's legacy of his or her early years, in his or her own words.

Set aside a bookshelf in your child's room for his or her books and journals, and reread them periodically with your child, the author.

## BOOST YOUR TEEN'S WRITING POWER

As a young teen, I often borrowed from the "diary" writing model. Today, they'd call me a "memoirist" or, much more likely (and much less charmingly), a "blogger."

No matter. Once I'd read *The Diary of Anne Frank*, I eagerly adopted her literary technique. I channeled Anne in book reports, creative essays, and history papers, using the "Dear Diary" format that had worked so well for her. If writing a report on *Gone with the Wind*, I'd pen a first-person account of life in the Civil War South. A history paper would inspire a personal journal chronicling D-Day or the Allies' victory march along the Champs-Elysées.

Some of these academic endeavors worked better than others. The good news? With considerable apologies to Descartes: I read, therefore I wrote.

We've already explored the way reading books (magazines, too!) shapes — make that *transforms* — the way young children learn to write. Reading works similar magic for middle school kids and young teens.

Yes, students can master writing basics in the classroom — topic sentence, introduction, body, and conclusion — and cobble together enough respectable reports to plod through the education system. But if you'd rather your child write with a measure of spirit, personality, insight, and self-awareness, head directly to the library — and take your teen with you.

Here's where you discover that selecting books for your teen does not even marginally resemble choosing books for your toddler. For those of you who have actually met a teenager, you'll immediately recognize the non sequitur in that last sentence: Let's face it, hardly anyone chooses books for their teen.

What you can do is conduct an unscientific survey of the books your kids spend time with, whether for school assignments or pure sprawling-across-the-bed reading pleasure.

Then pick up one or two of these books and read them. That's right: Read the latest *Maximum Ride* or *Camp Confidential* or even *The Chronicles of Narnia*. Some middle-schoolers might feel you've treaded on their precious, private print territory, but others will appreciate the fact that mom or dad is showing interest in their literary pursuits.

Reading — or at least getting up close and personal with your kids' book selections — gives you a way to initiate a dialogue with your teens about a book's plot, characters, and themes. For parents with a brainy bent, those talks can grow into discussions about technique, voice, and style: "What descriptive devices does the author use to set a scene?" "What new words have you come across?" "How would you emulate the author's style?"

## TIPS TALKING WITH YOUR TEEN ABOUT BOOKS

**Ask your teen:**

- What kind of book is this? (Romantic novel? Autobiography? Fantasy? Political thriller?)
- Does the author have a message he or she is trying to impart?
- What kinds of emotions do you feel as you read this book?
- Who is the reading audience the author has in mind for the book?
- What kind of research do you think the author did?
- What can you find out about the author's background?
- What "voice" does the writer use? (Narrative? First person? Humorous?)
- How does the author shape descriptive scenes? What literary devices does he or she use?
- In what other ways could the author have structured the plot? The characters? The ending?
- What ideas does this book give you if you were to write a story in this genre? What would you do differently?

My own daughter loved it when I read her books and shared thoughts and sentiments about classics such as *A Wrinkle in Time* by Madeleine L'Engle and the *Wizard of Oz* series. And the truth is, it was rather blissful revisiting these old friends — or in many cases, meeting them for the first time.

### It's all about vampires

In case you're wondering what today's kids consider compelling reading, check out any "top 10 books for teens" list. Most likely, you'll find a vampire in there somewhere: *Vampire Academy*, *Vampire Diaries*, and the hugely popular *Twilight* series, which got so hot, author Stephenie Meyer was dubbed the next J.K. Rowling.

Yes, vampires make for fun reading for teens and can be reasonably entertaining for grownups, too. And with a little creativity, parents and teachers can use these vampires' powers for good.

Kids devour romantic fantasy stories, so why not suggest that your middle-schooler write one? Help her structure a fantasy by discussing plot lines, setting, and characters. Where will the story take place? In space? Around the corner? How will the characters meet and fall in love?

Then suggest your teen sketch out an outline and structure it according to who the characters are, where they meet, and what happens to them. Maybe one of the characters possesses special powers or acquires them. At some point, the story should deal with problems or crises the characters must overcome.

Vampire tales can be exhilarating. Exposing your teenager to additional genres? Even better. An ample array of biographies, memoirs, poetry collections, historical novels, and classics line library and bookstore shelves (some suggested titles are in the "Resources" section at the end of this book). Browse through a collection with your teen. Help her make some choices. And encourage her to read critically and thoughtfully — and with an imagination that knows no bounds.

## PUBLIC SPEAKING: SHAKING STAGE FRIGHT

When I went through school, learning how to speak in public was a Very Big Deal. Kindergarten teachers launched show-and-tell. That grew into the one-minute oral book report, which became the three-minute "How I Spent My Summer" commentary. Those of us who discovered an inviting niche that combined unlimited verbosity with undivided attention forged ahead with speech and debate class.

That was then, this is now. Today's schools often tread water amid tight budgets, large classes, and revamped priorities. Parents, teachers, and students find agendas altered as educators and others lobby for courses in technology or life skills or global learning, or whatever politically, culturally, or educationally correct matrix those in charge deem worthy.

What's more, there's no public-speaking section on the SAT, the ACT, or any other standardized test. And in an era that quantifies learning, No Child Left Behind translates into No Way to Measure, which translates into No Way Schools Will Spend Time and Money Teaching It.

"There's a perception that using all the cool tech stuff will take the place of getting up and communicating your ideas verbally," says Joel Underwood, speech and debate coach at Seattle Academy of Arts and Science. "But actually, the opposite is true. People are impressed by those who can get up and speak well."

Can your youngster get up and speak — articulately, intelligently, and persuasively — if asked to do so?

### Communication skills matter

People base judgments about others on the way they speak and use language, Underwood points out. "Those skills — how to exchange ideas, how to have a discussion or a debate in a positive manner — that's what our kids aren't learning," he says.

Instead, they watch confrontation-style TV talk shows that pass for an exchange of ideas. "This *Crossfire*-type programming presents two people from far extremes who shout at each other," says Underwood. "Whoever yells the loudest wins."

But it's not just politicians who are called upon to publicly voice their views. Poets do readings; scientists give presentations; community organizers, board members, and corporate CEOs offer PowerPoint presentations. The truth is, just about every career path will, sooner or later, involve talking to (or in front of) people. "You need to know you will survive it," Underwood says.

Kids also need to know they'll survive interviews. Chances are, they'll face a few. There's the college interview, the job interview, and — you can always dream — the interview your daughter gives after she writes her best seller or wins the Tour de France.

**How to help**

How can you encourage your kids to become effective speakers? First, understand that many children — like many adults — may never be completely comfortable in front of a group. Be sensitive to those anxieties. If your child is about to deliver an oral report at school, he'll be nervous the night before. Make sure he has a good night's sleep and a good breakfast the next morning.

Volunteer to act as an audience for your child's practice speech. Be supportive, even if he stumbles over a word or two or trips over his shoelaces. And don't overcorrect — that's the teacher's job.

Then give him one tip — and one tip only — that you feel will enhance his presentation: Slow down. Keep breathing. Talk louder.

**TIPS PUBLIC SPEAKING**

- Make eye contact.
- Speak loudly.
- Use hand motions.
- Enhance the facts with a personal experience or story.
- Don't memorize your speech; it takes too much energy and increases anxiety. Use index cards or notes, if possible.
- Show interest and enthusiasm in your topic.
- Use props; these will help you feel people aren't staring at you.
- Don't speak in a monotone; vary your voice.
- Practice in front of a mirror.

Source: Dr. Kenneth Snyder, founder of Leaders of Tomorrow Foundation and co-author of *What! I Have to Give a Speech?*

As Underwood points out, "Your child will have all kinds of opportunities to speak. Maybe he'll give a talk at Boy Scouts, or she'll have a bat mitzvah. There's plenty of time to give lots of advice."

What else can you do? Model good communication at home. Encourage children to talk about their day around the dinner table and ask them specific questions. And remember that kids soak up verbal patterns, nuances, and plain old unattractive slang from their parents.

Find them outlets and activities, such as drama or glee club, that promote performing and speaking. And make sure they watch you deliver a talk or two in front of a group, even if it's just a family gathering. If you suffer a bit from public-speaking anxiety yourself, it's OK to initiate your own oratory career with the simplest of speeches: offer a toast. It's a beginning.

CHAPTER 10

# School's Out! Now What?

■ ■ ■ ■ ■

## STAYING SCHOOL SHARP DURING SUMMER

Who remembers summertime — a time when the livin' was easy and the burgers were grilling? Most of us must search deep into our memory banks for those wistful images of bicycle rides, walks in the park, and pickup games of sandlot baseball.

If you were born closer to the 21st century, you might have to review DVDs of *The Wonder Years* to really grasp those summer days of yore. Chances are, your busy parents wanted you active and supervised — and a safe distance from empty playgrounds and solitary trails.

Today, summer is the new fall: a time for fresh beginnings and infinite learning opportunities.

### A summer slide?

In a Web article titled "The Summer Brain Drain," the Family Education Network suggests parents consider the benefits of summer school or summer tutoring. "Summer school can enrich and accelerate learning in areas where kids show a special interest," states the article.

The Johns Hopkins University's Center for Summer Learning Web site weighs in with this view: "Summer 'slide' is another consequence of unstructured summers. The 'slide' means that students tend to score lower on tests of achievement at the end of the summer than they did on the same tests before summer break."

Many camps, as well as summer schools, provide learning opportunities in countless academic disciplines along with their usual menu of swimming, sports, and art.

No wonder so many parents are scrambling to enroll their kids in summer classes, math clubs, and science-enrichment camps. For students, that means less play and more skill building during the vacation months.

Is that such a bad thing?

Many educators think it's not, as long as kids strike a reasonable balance between mind building and mindless fun. "Summer is definitely a time for kids to explore interests and enjoy more freedom," says Sarah Shero, a former Seattle-area youth and recreation director. "But if they don't keep up with math and reading comprehension, they could lose up to six months of what they're learning. The goal in the summer is for kids to maintain their knowledge; it makes it easier on them when they get back to school."

And while kids shouldn't feel overly pressured during summer, they should always be learning, contends Uzma Merchant, owner of a Northwest branch of FasTracKids, an international education enrichment program. "You should expose them to as many things as you can."

**Combining play and learning**

Stowe Sprague, a mother of three children, ages nine, seven, and four, likes setting "summer goals" for her kids. "It might be as simple as learning to tie shoes," she says.

Tuned into her kids' strengths and weaknesses, she knows which child needs extra help in math, which in writing. Summertime, she finds, is a chance to jump on those weak spots and build them up. Sprague also values her children's downtime. "We're talking about fifteen to twenty minutes a day of reviewing," she says. "They have lots of time to play."

Sprague supplies the older kids with workbooks and texts, and makes sure they study at the kitchen counter while she prepares dinner. "They protest, but get into the swing," says Sprague. "I think of it as another version of quiet time."

That kind of formal structure is fine — if a child needs it, says Jeff Sanderson, math instructor and academic dean at Eastside Preparatory School in Kirkland, Washington. Sanderson sometimes assigns work over the summer if a student "fails to master" the material taught during the school year, he says. "But if they've done a pretty good job, they should have the summer off."

Sanderson suggests kids engage in enriching summer experiences that build on skills learned in the classroom, such as science or computer camps, or robotics.

What else keeps kids thinking? Journal writing, creative writing, and reading, he says. "While summer should be about play, the smart parent ties that play in with whatever the kids do during the school year." Taking a trip? Talk about what your child learned in social studies or history. Selecting books? Choose something that relates to science.

In fact, work and play aren't all that dissimilar, according to Frank Magusin, head of The Bush School in Seattle. Kids keep learning all the time. "There's a lot of processing that goes on during downtime, whether that time's spent reading magazines or creating rules for games," he says.

Some structured summer learning is not a bad thing, especially if a child wants to do it, says Magusin. But save time for fun. "I worry that we are overprogramming kids, and that there are not enough opportunities for them to play and learn how to be together," says Magusin. "It's really important to have time when kids can just be kids."

## MAKING THE MOST OF VACATION TIME

The flip-flops surface, daylight lingers, and the brilliant rays begin to peek through the gray. Summer's coming, and so is a common source of parental stress: How can I whip up the right balance of summertime experiences for the kids, one that will blend fun and learning with family time? Is there any upside to downtime?

Somewhere between baseball games, swim team, soccer camp, and Kumon class, there's a week or two that begs for the kind of old-fashioned "together" time we used to call "trips" and Expedia calls "Exciting Family Fun." And whether you spend that week unwinding at a nearby beach, or jetting off to Rome or Rio, you can make that time memorable and entertaining, all the while tossing a little knowledge and culture into the mix.

Stacy Winegardner is a big believer in using those "teachable moments." As education and exhibits director of KidsQuest, a children's museum near Seattle, Winegardner's expanded definition of "family vacation" includes spending quality "together" time at the park, or even in your own backyard.

"The main point is getting out as a family," she says. "We are surrounded by so many amazing things outside. There is so much knowledge kids can access without even realizing they are learning."

Winegardner sees educational opportunities in the kinds of natural objects most of us breeze right by: rocks, trees, seashells. Use these things as starting points for beginning-level earth science and ecology lessons, she suggests. "Talk to your kids about the way the moon can affect tides and the way moonlight can affect seas," she says. "You don't have to go to a science center to do that."

Traveling on a ferry? Talk about boats, study the ferry maps, and discuss transportation. Study ports and the way they work. Kids might like to know the different ways goods are transported, and how we get the shoes and the video games we buy at the store.

Set what Debbie Kray of the Children's Museum of Tacoma, Washington, calls "summer learning goals." It can be as simple as talking about planting a family garden. "Have the kids research plants or seeds, or do the math about planting times and chart growth," says Kray. "And you don't have to let them know they're doing 'summer learning.'"

### Big trips

If you're lucky enough to be taking a Big Trip — and anything out of your state qualifies as one — you might want to put in some prep time. Read books with your child about your trip destination, help create a budget, or calculate what the daily expenses will be.

Don't underestimate the power of film. It's fun to watch movies set in your destination — think *An American in Paris* — and kids absorb cultural and historical ingredients (baguettes? Gershwin?) whether they're trying to or not.

My children were twelve and fifteen on their first trip to Israel. In a perfect world, they'd have devoured *Exodus* by Leon Uris, all 608 pages of it. I had to settle for the two of them gazing at the 208-minute screen version that stars Paul Newman. All things considered, it wasn't a terrible trade-off.

The pretrip reading list need not be limited to Fodor's. From *The Diary of Anne Frank* to *Mary Poppins*, children can visualize culture, geography, and history as reflected through fiction, narratives, and biographies.

What else can you do together? Pore over maps and ask the kids to help plan routes. Compute distances and time frames. How long will it take to get from point A to point B? How will you get there: by plane, train, or automobile?

### How to fly

My own family settled on planes as the mode of transportation that worked best, after several unfortunate (if not dangerous) liaisons with trains and automobiles. That generally meant coming up with a solid strategic plan to make flying reasonably pleasant and somewhat relaxing.

#### TIPS TRAVELING WITH KIDS

- Think about places you'd like to visit, then cut out two-thirds of them. Concentrate on a few areas and really get to know them.
- Visit two places in two weeks. The younger the child, the fewer places you should visit.
- Do the little things with kids, not the big things. Watch people make cheese. Stop in small villages and towns. Visit castles, look at the cobblestone roads, watch the swans in the park.
- Learning experiences are everywhere in a foreign country. There's probably another language being spoken. Maybe stores close at 1 p.m. Help your child see the things that are done differently.
- Preparing for a trip, living it, and reliving it afterward are of equal value. When kids keep journals, their "after" experience will be much better. Another option: Take a video camera along and ask your child to talk into it, or assemble a post-trip scrapbook, complete with photos, descriptions, and assorted small mementos.
- The more flexible you are, the more fun your trip will be. Let things happen. If your children really like a place, stay there. You may not get the exact hotel you want, but you should be able to find a place to stay.

Source: Bob Ellis, instructor at the International School in Bellevue, Washington

For us, not the kids. What we wanted for them was a smidgen of learning and productivity to accompany the twelve bags of jelly beans we'd typically — and rather desperately — provide.

So along with the Legos, the puzzles, and the dot-to-dot drawing pads, we'd carry children's books filled with photos and descriptions of our destinations. I'd pack games, crayons, an Etch a Sketch, and plenty of paper, and wrap everything individually so the kids could open "surprises" every hour of the voyage. This was before 9/11, when you could tote a wrapped gift through security (if you try this today, leave the top of the wrapping open for inspection). We also gave the kids journals, optimistically hoping they'd scribble, draw, or even write in them.

The truth is, we improvised; there wasn't all that much out there in those days for travelin' tots.

Oh, how things have changed.

For starters, there's the portable DVD player. Yes, I said "DVD player." Take one on those mind-numbing, snackless, jam-packed, cheerless flights — you'll need it. These days, hapless parents struggle through terminals lugging the car seat and the stroller, stressing about the way they've packed up the breast milk and wondering whether the stuffed teddy bear will clear security. So borrow or buy the DVDs and make sure you chose high-quality films, such as Disney classics or, for young kids, LeapFrog learning programs.

On long flights, limit screen use and pull out the props. Pack "secret activity bags" and fill each with arts and crafts supplies, or books that include reusable stickers that the kids can use throughout the flight. Magnetic storyboards also work well on planes — they're self-contained and easy to pack.

Sue Nevins, who sells children's books at the Elliott Bay Book Company in Seattle, recommends toting along "Chicken Socks" activity books by Klutz. One of her favorites, *Totally Tape*, is perfect for young flyers, she says. It comes with four rolls of colorful paper tape and "tape me" pages; kids match shapes, create designs, or "paint" the pictures in tape.

Nevins also suggests bringing or downloading recorded books, such as those read by storyteller Jim Weiss. Titles include *Uncle Wiggly's Storybook, Animal Tales,* and *The Adventures of Tom Sawyer.*

However you get to wherever it is you're going, let your children be key planning participants. French instructor Bob Ellis, who teaches at the International School in Bellevue, Washington, leads students on visits to France. The parent of three sons, Ellis, along with his wife, also leads family visits to Europe. He likes to give his kids, both his students and his own children, a say in where they go.

He advises other parents, even parents of small children, to do the same. "If a four-year-old is interested in seeing the cows in Switzerland because he's looked at pictures of them in a book, then that's what you should go see," he says.

# A Final Note

Acting as a child's friend, mentor, advocate, and — most crucial of all — parent can be at once exhilarating, frustrating, and immensely rewarding. We know it's essential to be in the loop and involved, and to make sure our children make the most of the learning opportunities open to them. A 2002 report published by the Southwest Educational Development Laboratory (SEDL) found that families can improve their children's overall academic performance in school. "Families also have a major impact on other key outcomes, such as attendance and behavior, that affect achievement," the study reports.

So stay engaged; keep close watch over your kids' emotional and social growth, as well as their progress inside the classroom. Connect with the parenting community around you; nothing beats bouncing ideas, disappointments, and triumphs off other moms, dads, and caretakers. Visit online blogs and parent chat rooms, and check out local parenting magazines. And all the while, keep your eye on the prize: your own well-nurtured, well-prepared child.

View this as a responsibility, a challenge, and a privilege. My hope is that this book has provided you with the insights and tools that will help you gear up for that task, and that it will maximize your kids' chances for success, in school, in life, and perhaps one day, in their own parenting.

# Resources

## BOOKS

### Early learning

Gopnik, Alison, Andrew N. Meltzoff, and Patricia K. Kuhl. *The Scientist in the Crib: What Early Learning Tells Us About the Mind.* Harper, 2000.

Hirsh-Pasek, Kathy, Roberta Michnick Golinkoff, and Diane Eyer. *Einstein Never Used Flashcards.* Rodale Books, 2004.

Singer, Dorothy G., Roberta Michnick Golinkoff, and Kathy Hirsh-Pasek. *Play = Learning.* Oxford University Press, 2006.

### School issues

Carter, Margie, Deb Curtis, Brenda Hieronymus, and Elizabeth Jones. *Training Teachers: A Harvest of Theory and Practice.* Redleaf Press, 2002.

Davis, Stan. *Schools Where Everyone Belongs: Practical Strategies for Reducing Bullying.* Research Press, 2007.

Holbrook, Sara and Michael Salinger. *Outspoken! How to Improve Writing and Speaking Skills Through Poetry Performance.* Heinemann, 2006.

Kohn, Alfie. *The Homework Myth: Why Our Kids Get Too Much of a Bad Thing.* Da Capo Press, 2007.

Levine, Gail Carson. *Writing Magic: Creating Stories That Fly.* Collins, 2006.

Sheras, Peter. *Your Child: Bully or Victim? Understanding and Ending Schoolyard Tyranny.* Fireside, 2002.

Silbert, Linda Bress, and Alvin J. Silbert. *Why Bad Grades Happen to Good Kids.* Beaufort Books, 2007.

Snyder, Kenneth, and Thomas J. Murphy. *What! I Have to Give a Speech?* The Family Learning Association, 2002.

Thompson, Michael and Theresa Barker. *The Pressured Child: Helping Your Child Find Success in School and Life.* Ballantine, 2005.

### Giftedness

*Early Gifts: Recognizing and Nurturing Children's Talents.* Edited by Paula Olszewski-Kubilius, Lisa Limburg-Weber, and Steven Pfeiffer. Prufrock Press Inc., 2003.

Palmer, David. *Parents' Guide to IQ Testing and Gifted Education.* Parent Guide Books, 2006.

### Gender issues

Gurian, Michael. *Boys and Girls Learn Differently!* Jossey-Bass, 2001.

Gurian, Michael. *The Purpose of Boys.* Jossey-Bass, 2009.

Gurian, Michael. *The Wonder of Girls.* Atria, 2003.

Kindlon, Dan, and Michael Thompson. *Raising Cain: Protecting the Emotional Life of Boys.* Ballantine Books, 2000.

Simmons, Rachel. *Odd Girl Out: The Hidden Culture of Aggression in Girls.* Harvest Books, 2003.

Wiseman, Rosalind. *Queen Bees and Wannabes: Helping Your Daughter Survive Cliques, Gossip, Boyfriends, and Other Realities of Adolescence.* Three Rivers Press, 2003.

### Social and emotional growth

Borba, Michele. *Building Moral Intelligence: The Seven Essential Virtues that Teach Kids to Do the Right Thing.* Jossey-Bass, 2001.

Goleman, Daniel. *Emotional Intelligence.* Bantam Books, 1995.

Gottman, John, and Joan Declaire. *Raising an Emotionally Intelligent Child.* Simon & Schuster, 1998.

Kabat-Zinn, Myla, and Jon Kabat-Zinn. *Everyday Blessings: The Inner Work of Mindful Parenting.* Hyperion, 1998.

Levine, David A. *Teaching Empathy: A Blueprint for Caring, Compassion, and Community.* Solution Tree, 2005.

Rubin, Kenneth H. *The Friendship Factor.* Penguin Books, 2002.

### Nutrition

Pressey, Beverly. *Simple & Savvy Strategies for Creating Healthy Eaters.* Two Harbors Press, 2008.

Waters, Alice L. *Edible Schoolyard: A Universal Idea.* Chronicle Books, 2008.

Waters, Alice L. *Fanny at Chez Panisse: A Child's Restaurant Adventures with 46 Recipes.* William Morrow Cookbooks, 1997.

Woolley, Janice W., and Jennifer Pugmire. *Food for Tots.* Mammoth Prints, 2001.

### General parenting

Borba, Michele. *The Big Book of Parenting Solutions: 101 Answers to Your Everyday Challenges and Wildest Worries.* Jossey-Bass, 2009.

Crary, Elizabeth. *Love & Limits: Guidance Tools for Creative Parenting.* Parenting Press, 1994.

Dweck, Carol. *Mindset: The New Psycholgy of Success.* Random House, 2006.

Elkind, David. *The Power of Play: Learning What Comes Naturally.* Da Capo Press, 2006.

Karp, Harvey. *The Happiest Baby on the Block: The New Way to Calm Crying and Help Your Newborn Baby Sleep Longer.* Bantam, 2003.

Karp, Harvey. *The Happiest Toddler on the Block: The New Way to Stop the Daily Battle of Wills and Raise a Secure and Well-Behaved One- to Four-Year-Old.* Bantam, 2008.

Kastner, Laura S., and Jennifer F. Wyatt. *The Seven-Year Stretch: How Families Work Together to Grow Through Adolescence.* Houghton Mifflin, 1997.

Kastner, Laura S., and Jennifer F. Wyatt. *Getting to Calm: Cool-headed Strategies for Parenting Tweens and Teens.* ParentMap Books, 2009.

Kohn, Alfie. *Unconditional Parenting: Moving from Rewards and Punishments to Love and Reason.* Atria, 2006.

Mogel, Wendy. *The Blessing of a Skinned Knee: Using Jewish Teachings to Raise Self-Reliant Children.* Scribner, 2001.

Siegel, Daniel J., and Mary Hartzell. *Parenting from the Inside Out.* Jeremy P. Tarcher/Penguin, 2003.

**Web sites**

Alliance for Childhood
*allianceforchildhood.net*
P.O. Box 444, College Park, MD 20741
301-779-1033

Association for Women in Science
*awis.org*
1200 New York Ave. N.W., Suite 650, Washington, DC 20005
202-326-8940

Committee for Children
*cfchildren.org*
568 First Ave. S., Suite 600, Seattle, WA 98104
800-634-4449, ext. 6223

DreamBox Learning
*dreambox.com*
10900 N.E. Eighth St., Suite 600, Bellevue, WA 98004
425-637-8900

Expanding Your Horizons in Science and Mathematics
*expandingyourhorizons.org*
The Expanding Your Horizons Network
Mills College
5000 MacArthur Blvd., Oakland, CA 94613
510-430-2222

Foundation for Early Learning
*earlylearning.org*
615 Second Ave., Suite 525, Seattle, WA 98104
206-525-4801

Giant Campus
*giantcampus.com*
3131 Elliott Ave., Suite 790, Seattle, WA 98121
800-968-1368

Gottman Institute
*gottman.com*
P.O. Box 15644, Seattle, WA 98115-0644
888-523-9042

Institute for Learning and Brain Sciences
*ilabs.washington.edu*
Box 357988
University of Washington, Seattle, WA 98195-7988
206-543-6000

Johns Hopkins University Center for Talented Youth
*cty.jhu.edu*
McAuley Hall
5801 Smith Ave., Suite 400, Baltimore, MD 21209
410-735-4100

National Association for Gifted Children
*nagc.org*
1707 L St. N.W., Suite 550, Washington, DC 20036
202-785-4268

National Association for the Education of Young Children (NAEYC)
*naeyc.org*
1313 L St. N.W., Suite 500, Washington, DC 20005
800-424-2460

National Child Care Information and Technical Assistance Center
*nccic.acf.hhs.gov/index.cfm*
10530 Rosehaven St., Suite 400, Fairfax, VA 22030
800-616-2242

National Center for Learning Disabilities
*ncld.org*
381 Park Ave. S., Suite 1401, New York, NY 10016
212-545-7510, 888-575-7373

National Education Association
*nea.org*
1201 16th St. N.W., Washington, DC 20036-3290
202-833-4000

Roots of Empathy
*rootsofempathy.org*
250 Ferrand Drive, Suite 800
Toronto, ON Canada, M3C 3G8
416-944-3001

Talaris Institute
*talaris.org*
P.O. Box 45040, Seattle, WA 98145
206-859-5600

U.S. Department of Education
*ed.gov/parents/landing.jhtml*
400 Maryland Ave. S.W., Washington, DC 20202
800-872-5327

Zero to Three
*zerotothree.org*
National Center for Infants, Toddlers and Families
2000 M St. N.W., Suite 200, Washington, DC 20036
202-638-1144

## RECOMMENDED READING FOR CHILDREN

Recommended by Maria Pontillas, youth services librarian at the Tacoma Public Library in Washington.

### Elementary school

*A Couple of Boys Have the Best Week Ever* by Marla Frazee
Two young boys, Eamon and James, spend an action-packed weekend at Eamon's grandparents' beach cottage in this lively picture book.

*The Foggy, Foggy Forest* by Nick Sharratt
What's going on in the forest? Opaque pages keep kids guessing as famous storybook characters frolic between the pages of this picture book.

*The Doghouse* by Jan Thomas
When the ball accidentally goes into the doghouse, Mouse sends his friends in one by one to retrieve it. But they don't come out. Will Mouse be next? A silly picture book just right for sharing.

*Savvy* by Ingrid Law
Mibs Beaumont's thirteenth birthday will be special. Thirteen is the year that the Beaumont kids get their savvy, or special talent. One brother creates electricity, another commands hurricanes. What will Mibs' savvy be?

*Maze of Bones* by Rick Riordan
Siblings Amy and Dan are heartbroken when their grandmother dies, but at her funeral they are invited to enter a game that promises world domination to the winner. They embark on a worldwide challenge to chase down the 39 clues and defend the family name. First book in the "39 Clues" series.

## Middle school

*The Underneath* by Kathi Appelt
Part legend, part love story, part animal tale, this is the unforgettable story of an old dog named Ranger and three abandoned cats who live under a rickety house in the swamp. When they are separated by Ranger's cruel owner, the animals struggle to be reunited.

*Invasion of the Road Weenies* by David Lubar
Like *The Twilight Zone* for kids, this book is filled with creepy, funny, and just plain weird short stories.

*Waiting for Normal* by Leslie Connor
Twelve-year-old Addie just wants a normal life. Her mother is busy with new business ideas and boyfriends. Her mom's ex-husband, Dwight, has his own family to take care of. Who has time for Addie?

*The Mysterious Benedict Society* by Trenton Lee Stewart
Answering an ad, talented orphan Reynie Muldoon joins three other special children to form the Mysterious Benedict Society. They are sent on a special mission to infiltrate the Learning Institute for the Very Enlightened. A *Lemony Snicket*–inspired adventure.

*Middle School Is Worse Than Meatloaf* by Jennifer L. Holm
As told through diary entries, notes, and class schedules, seventh-grader Ginny Davis is having a hard time adjusting to middle school. Her former best friend got the lead in the ballet, Brian Bukvic keeps bothering her, and her juvenile-delinquent brother might have pulled his last prank ever.

*What the World Eats* by Faith D'Aluisio and Peter Menzel
Ever wonder what families in Egypt eat? Flip through this book, which features photos and facts about kitchens, cooking, and food from all over the world.

## High school

*What I Saw and How I Lied* by Judy Blundell
When sixteen-year-old Evie's stepdad Joe returns from WWII, life goes back to normal, but one day a mysterious phone call sends the family to Florida. There, a handsome ex-soldier catches Evie's eye, but he seems to make Joe nervous. Sometimes things are not what they seem.

*The Hunger Games* by Suzanne Collins
If you like watching "Survivor," you'll love this book! Sixteen-year-old Katniss gets a chance to save her family from a life of poverty when she is randomly chosen to participate in the Hunger Games, a competition that pits kids against each other in a fight to the death.

*Little Brother* by Cory Doctorow
When terrorists blow up a bridge in San Francisco, seventeen-year-old Marcus and his friends are kidnapped and cruelly questioned by the police as suspects. Now the government is watching their every move.

**More titles for teens**

*A Child Called "It": One Child's Courage to Survive* by David J. Pelzer
*A Maze Me: Poems for Girls* by Naomi Shihab Nye
*The Alchemist* by Paulo Coelho
*Angela's Ashes* by Frank McCourt
*Bee Season* by Myla Goldberg
*The Bell Jar* by Sylvia Plath
*Beloved* by Toni Morrison
*Bras and Broomsticks* by Sarah Mlynowski
*Breakfast at Tiffany's* by Truman Capote
*Breaking Dawn* by Stephenie Meyer
*The Chosen* by Chaim Potok
*Cold Sassy Tree* by Olive Ann Burns
*Great Expectations* by Charles Dickens
*The Heart Is a Lonely Hunter* by Carson McCullers
*Into Thin Air* by Jon Krakauer
*I Know Why the Caged Bird Sings* by Maya Angelou
*Light-Gathering Poems,* edited by Liz Rosenberg, by various poets
*The Story of My Life* by Helen Keller
*Tuesdays with Morrie* by Mitch Albom
*Up from Slavery* by Booker T. Washington

# Index

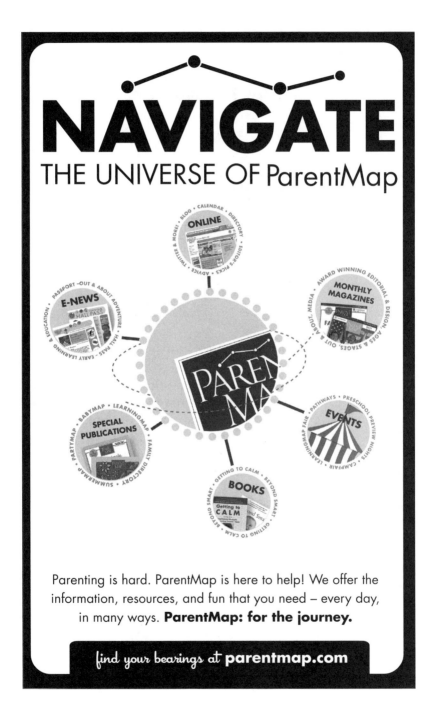

# About the Author

MICHAEL MORGAN

Linda Morgan, a Seattle-area writer and editor, is a former college communications and journalism instructor, and the education editor of *ParentMap*, an award-winning Northwest parenting publication. She discusses educational issues regularly on NBC's Seattle affiliate station. A Phi Beta Kappa graduate of the University of California at Berkeley, with a master's degree in journalism from UCLA, she has been recognized both regionally and nationally with numerous journalism awards. Morgan lives on Mercer Island, Washington, with her husband, Michael.